The
Mentored
Life

The
Mentored
Life

*From Individualism
to Personhood*

James M. Houston

REGENT COLLEGE PUBLISHING
Vancouver, British Columbia

First published 2002 by NavPress, PO Box 35001, Colorado Springs, CO 80935 U.S.A.

This edition published 2012 by
Regent College Publishing
5800 University Boulevard
Vancouver, BC V6T 2E4 Canada
Web: www.regentpublishing.com
E-mail: info@regentpublishing.com

Regent College Publishing is an imprint of the Regent Bookstore <www.regentbookstore.com>.
Views expressed in works published by Regent College Publishing are those of the author and do
not necessarily represent the official position of Regent College <www.regent-college.edu>.

Some of the anecdotal illustrations in this book are true to life and are included with the
permission of the persons involved. All other illustrations are composites of real situations, and any
resemblance to people living or dead is coincidental.

Unless otherwise noted, Scripture quotations are taken from the *Holy Bible, New International
Version*®. NIV®. Copyright © 1973, 1978, 1984 by International Bible Society. Used by permission
of Zondervan. All rights reserved. Scripture quotations marked KJV are taken from the King
James Version. (Public Domain.) Italics in Scripture have been used by the author for emphasis;
NASB are taken from the *New American Standard Bible*, © Copyright 1960, 1995 by the Lockman
Foundation. Used by permission; and ESV are taken from the *The Holy Bible, English Standard
Version*. Copyright 2000, 2001 by Crossway Bibles, a division of Good News Publishers. Used by
permission. All rights reserved.

Library and Archives Canada Cataloguing in Publication Data

Houston, J. M. (James Macintosh), 1922–
     The mentored life / James M. Houston.

Includes bibliographical references.
     ISBN 978-1-57383-447-6

     1. Mentoring in church work. I. Title.

BV4408.5.H69 2010   253'.7   C2010-905083-5

To Peter Shaw, Sandra Sharpe, and all subsequent alumni of Regent College and the C. S. Lewis Institute, who inspired and taught me the contents of this book

CONTENTS

/

INTRODUCTION

BY DALLAS WILLARD

James Houston presents discipleship to Jesus Christ as the greatest opportunity individual human beings have in life and the only hope corporate mankind has of solving its insurmountable problems.

Discipleship affirms the unity of the present-day Christian with those who walked beside Jesus during His incarnation. To be His disciple then was to be with Him, to learn to be like Him. It was to be His student or apprentice in kingdom living. His disciples heard what He said and observed what He did, then, under His direction, they simply began to say and do the same things. They did so imperfectly but progressively. As He taught: "Everyone who is fully trained will be like his teacher" (Luke 6:40).

Today it is the same, except now it is the resurrected Lord who walks throughout the world. He invites us to place our confidence in Him. Those who rely on Him believe that He knows how to live and will pour His life into us as we take His yoke and learn from Him, for He is "gentle and humble in heart" (Matt. 11:29). To take His yoke means joining Him in His work, making our work His work. To trust Him is to understand that total immersion in what He is doing with our life is the best thing that could ever happen to us.

To "learn from Him" in this total-life immersion is how we "seek first his kingdom and his righteousness" (Matt. 6:33). The outcome is that we increasingly are able to do all things, speaking or acting, as if Christ were doing them (Col. 3:17). As apprentices of Christ we are not learning how to do some special religious activity, but how to live every moment of our lives from the reality of God's kingdom. I am learning how to live my actual life as Jesus would if He were me.

If I am a plumber, clerk, bank manager, homemaker, elected official, senior citizen, or migrant worker, I am in "full-time" Christian service no less than someone who earns his or her living in a specifically religious role. Jesus stands beside me and teaches me in all I do to live in God's world. He shows me how, in every circumstance, to reside in His Word and thus be a genuine apprentice of His—His disciple indeed. This enables me to find the reality of God's world everywhere I may be, and thereby to escape from enslavement to sin and evil (John 8:31–32). We become able to do what we know to be good and right, even when it is humanly impossible. Our lives and words become constant testimony of the reality of God.

A plumber facing a difficult plumbing job must know how to integrate it into the kingdom of God as much as someone attempting to win another to Christ or preparing a lesson for a congregation. Until we are clear on this, we will have missed Jesus' connection between life and God and will automatically exclude most of our everyday lives from the domain of faith and discipleship. Jesus lived most of His life on earth as a blue-collar worker, someone we might describe today as an "independent contractor." In His vocation He practiced everything He later taught about life in the kingdom.

The "words" of Jesus I primarily reside in are those recorded in the New Testament Gospels. In His presence, I learn the goodness of His instructions and how to carry them out. It is not a matter of meriting life from above, but of receiving that life concretely in my circumstances. Grace, we must learn, is opposed to earning, not to effort.

For example, I move away from using derogatory language against others, calling them twits, jerks, or idiots (Matt. 5:22), and increasingly mesh with the respect and endearment for persons that naturally flows from God's way. This in turn transforms all of my dealings with others into tenderness and makes the usual coldness and brutality of human relations, which lays a natural foundation for abuse and murder, simply unthinkable.

Of course, the "learning of Him" is meant to occur in the context of His people. They are the ones He commissioned to make disciples, surround them in the reality of the triune name, and teach to do "everything I have commanded you" (Matt. 28:20). But the disciples we make are His disciples, never ours. We are His apprentices along with them. If we are a little further along the way, we can only echo the apostle Paul: "Follow my example, as I follow the example of Christ" (1 Cor. 11:1).

It is a primary task of Christian ministry today, and of those who write for this line of books, to reestablish Christ as a living teacher in the midst of His people. He has been removed by various historical developments: assigned the role of mere sacrifice for sin or social prophet and martyr. But where there is no teacher, there can be no students or disciples.

If we cannot be His students, we have no way to learn

to exist always and everywhere within the riches and power of His Word. We can only flounder along as if we were on our own so far as the actual details of our lives are concerned. That is where multitudes of well-meaning believers find themselves today. But it is not the intent of Him who says, "Come to me.... and you will find rest for your souls" (Matt. 11:28–29).

Each book in this line is designed to contribute to this renewed vision of Christian spiritual formation and to illuminate what apprenticeship to Jesus Christ means within all the specific dimensions of human existence. The mission of these books is to form the whole person so that the nature of Christ becomes the natural expression of our souls, bodies, and spirits throughout our daily lives.

—*Dallas Willard*

If one falls down, his friend can help him up.
But pity the man who falls and has no one to help him up!
—Ecclesiastes 4:10

A human being's highest achievement is to let God
be able to help him.
—Søren Kierkegaard

FOREWORD

This book is about house building after a disastrous flood or earthquake. But the house is not a roof over our heads; it is inside us. It is what constitutes you and me. It is about our individual identities. Since the 1960s, we have been living through vast cultural changes, which, like a flood or earthquake, have destroyed many of our traditional values—as well as our self-understanding. We live also after September 11, 2001. So we look at the rubble, we see the various stages of how and when the "house" of "the self" has been built up, and we see how faulty were the foundations. And now we must rebuild.

It is my hope that by the end of the book we may have learned to distinguish how to build "upon the rock," as Jesus taught, and no longer "upon the sands." This will not be easy reading, for it challenges a change of mind-set and offers a new way of living.

In our intensely individualistic society today, we tend to forget we are social beings. Ours has become a ruinous culture when we behave and act so autonomously as individuals. Yet simple reflection should remind us how multiple is "the Other," even within ourselves. You and I live with bodies. We live as a man or woman. I even talk frequently to myself. Supremely, I have to live before God as the transcendent Other, or at least to be aware of the social reality beyond myself. These differing "others" in my life all contradict the illusion of "living by myself" or of seeking a "self-fulfilled life."

Ecologists remind us that a tree planted in a clearing of an old forest will grow more successfully than when it is planted in isolation in an open field. The roots of the new planting will follow more easily and more deeply the hidden pathways of old root systems.[1] Likewise, human beings thrive best in following the paths of life already taken by others before them. None of us needs to reinvent the wheel or live as if no one has preceded us in the pathways of the wise. We learn best and grow most fully personally when we learn and develop socially; for beyond our own horizons there are those who have seen beyond us or have anticipated challenges and obstacles we may not yet have encountered on life's journey.

Ethically, too, my behavior lies in having to consider other people. In all these relationships, I need to be "mentored" to learn to appreciate "the Other" in my life, so that I do not become autistic or even selfish and self-centered. We may speak of mentoring as the process of "othering," when we become appreciative of the educational wealth other people can give us, as well as the social skills they challenge and help us to develop.

Modern-Day Mentoring

Despite its strong individualistic streak, secular society is becoming aware that mentoring can provide a corrective to the introverted self. Moreover, as our technical world becomes increasingly more complex, learning has become recognized as an ongoing process throughout life. We can continue to accumulate skills in an ever-expanding universe of specialized forms of knowledge.[2] Learning, instead of being viewed as a classroom situation limited to childhood, now is described as a journey—even an "interactive" one with other companions who act as "coaches," as "challengers," even as "long-distance mentors."

Modern communication skills for deepening the learning process now involve many more relational skills, such as listening, providing structures, raising positive expectations, sharing oneself, setting tasks and goals, modeling, mirroring, sustaining a tradition, shaping character, fostering self-reflection and respect for others, building trust, and indeed many more. Effective businesses now view their skilled employees as their greatest resource for the establishment of "intelligent organizations." *Feedback* has become a new buzzword within such dynamic interaction: "asking for feedback," "giving it," "receiving it," and "acting on feedback." Ultimately, the best employees are not simply those with proven technical skills, but those who demonstrate the most "personal growth" that is wholly committed to their employers. Along with a company's "profitability," then, is the "effectiveness" of its labor force, as demonstrated now by the investment in its mentoring skills.

Those who have commercialized mentoring actually first took notice of the effectiveness of the model of the sports coach. The same effectiveness is cultivated among team players learning to be strategists of their games and boosters of team morale. For often-overburdened public educators, mentoring, too, is being seen as an important new form of social assistance. It traditionally has been done by such programs as the Boy Scouts and Girl Scouts, Big Brothers and Big Sisters, Outward Bound, 4-H, and so on. The growing trend toward internships has also contributed to more specialized training. Likewise, the social ills of society are providing many volunteer opportunities for mentors.

Thus modern-day mentoring has become a vastly expanding sphere of social engagements, having both philosophical and pragmatic concerns within Western society. It is being viewed as creating positive benefits in a broadening spectrum of applications.[3] Like the popularity of "spirituality," which would extend human concerns beyond the rational, so mentoring reminds us of the effectiveness of being relational beings and of the need to network together.

THE ULTIMACY OF "PERSONHOOD"

Perhaps a central mystery of our humanness is that we are both individuals and social selves at the same time. Aristotelian thinking has made too much of the self as an individual substance. In overreaction some personalists—philosophers concerned with the personal character of the human being—put too much emphasis upon our relational identity. We are uniquely a self and yet also a self-in-relationships. However, this debate can be explored only within a Christian framework, because only the triune God of grace can provide a metaphysics for the ultimacy of "personhood." That is why we speak of "person(s)" as being a theological category. Only God in the Man-Christ, through His Spirit, can deliver us from our sinful or autonomous self to disciple us truly. Yet it is only the present cultural prominence being given to the role of the mentor today that now forces the thoughtful Christian to be alert to the false forms of mentoring and their motives, which are now proliferating.

As a Xhosa saying puts it, *Umuntu ngumuntu ngabantu* (Persons depend on other persons to be persons).[4] This is what the Christian life is about—building relationships upon the Rock, that is, upon the "Person-eity" of God's own nature, in His relationship with human beings.

Finding the Authentic Mentor

Becoming a Christian is a demolition of one's identity from the ruins of self-enclosures as being individualistic— literally "inhuman"—whereas to be human is to be a social being. Instead, one becomes more "open," not only to other people, but also to become radically reconstituted as a "person-in-Christ." How such an identity as a Christian disciple is differentiated from contemporary forms of the "mentored self" is then the underlying concern of this book.

This is not a "how-to" manual on ways to find a more established person to talk to and learn from. We will look at social influences—good and bad—that explicitly we relate to as mentors and mentoring systems. Some "mentor" from false premises; others—set within the Christian faith—may still be intensely individualistic, for they have not discerned the false cultural influence they have inherited. Depicted on the broad horizon of Western civilization, we may even call these "metamentoring" approaches to life that have shaped significantly our shared cultural heritage. How can we discern the good and the bad, the wise and the foolish, the true and the false among them? In a culture of confusion, as ours has become with pluralism, syncretism, and reductionism all so pervasive, it is hard to know how to be guided wisely.

This is the purpose of this book: to explore how the Christian finds the authentic Mentor or "Other" in his or her life.

Guidance for a Confused Generation

I have devoted my life to mentoring, first as an Oxford don for twenty-five years, teaching in a secular environment, and then for another thirty years at Regent College among theological students. It has been an enriching life, in deliberately choosing to be a facilitator of the hearts and minds of others rather than following the practice of more conventional understandings of "Christian leadership." Yet it is becoming increasingly apparent that there are great, widening differences among Christians themselves concerning attitudes and objectives for Christian life and service. The Christian identity perhaps has never been more confused, and this is cause of utmost concern.

This concern also motivates me to write this book: to give some illumination and guidance today for a confused generation of Christians who seek a genuine Christian identity. For this great task I identify with Søren Kierkegaard (1813–1855) when he said, "Before God, I regard my whole work as an author as my own education. I am not a teacher but a learner."5

Indeed, acknowledgments are the alter ego of our lives, as this book spells out. For that reason this book is dedicated to all my alumni who have taught me so much in helping me to persist in the transition from truth being just "thought" to becoming "life." I have learned to interpret the knock at my office door, not as an interruption, but as a fresh opportunity to learn more of the mysteries of our humanity.

Specifically I acknowledge the help of my teaching assistants Ken N. Pearson and Julie Canlis in filing my teaching materials; preliminary editorial help from Sharon

Jebb, Jude Fredericsen, and Mark Filiatreau; and the computer skills of Daniel Niles, Diane Krusemark, and my grandson Stephen Taylor, who saved me from many a logjam on my laptop. I am deeply indebted to Don Simpson, acquisitions editor at NavPress, who believed in my writing project, and for the critical and enlightening editing skills of Anita Palmer of Sam Hill Editorial Services, Nanci McAlister, Amy Spencer, and the other editorial staff of NavPress. The defects, which undoubtedly remain, lie only at my door. Profoundly, I am continually indebted to my wife, Rita, who has sacrificed her evenings with me to allow time for study as my way of life. Her hospitality to students for almost fifty years now has been the basis for the reflections of this book.

—James M. Houston
All Souls' Day, 2001

*Oneself as Another suggests from the outset that the selfhood of
oneself implies otherness to such an intimate degree
that one cannot be thought of without the other.*[1]

—Paul Ricoeur

OVERVIEW: MODERN MENTORING AND METAETHICAL SYSTEMS

OUR CULTURAL SEARCH FOR MENTORS

Mentors have been around perhaps as long as the human race. Shamans and witch doctors, prophets and philosophers, leaders and teachers go back deep into our history. Moses and Joshua, Confucius and Mencius, Socrates and Plato, Hillel and the Pharisees, have all transmitted their ways of life from teacher to pupil, mentor to mentee. Thus the minds of great thinkers have been passed from generation to generation. Their efficacy as teachers also has been in being exemplars, providing a way of life that could be imitated in deed as well as thought.

However, modern rationalism eclipsed their significance with "grand rational narratives" that no longer narrate to us, as if "truth" and "life" were independent identities. Now disenchanted by such disembodied generalizations, our age is looking for the exemplars of truth as a way of life. When the architects of modern life have frequently been such poor samples of humanity, we become disenchanted with their inconsistencies.

Alienation in Modern Society

Thus the fact that mentors are now being prominently sought reflects first upon the alienation of our age. It also reveals an indifference to history and past traditions, for we forget today the long tradition of apprenticeship that was the basis of craftsmanship and of the role played by elders in many societies.

"Fixers," not Friends

Second, when we are looking for help from the right kind of people, "fixers" or even "teachers" are not enough. Living in a technological society, we tend to reduce everything to instrumental knowledge that "fixes" everything. But techniques cannot be a substitute for wise companionship. We miss "the presence of the Other" in a technical world. We also live in an information society where knowledge is readily confused with "thinking about things." We forget that the nurturing and caring relationship is inherent in effective teaching. Wisdom, after all, is much more than data processing. Activism that is devoted to a cause can also be a poor substitute for relationships, becoming too "busy" to cultivate friends. The Greek philosophers were wiser when they stated that "thought is not meaningful without action; and action is not meaningful without friendship." When a teacher acts kindly as a friend, the pupil is given much more encouragement and trust in the learning relationship. Wisdom, personified in a mentor, is thus the way of excellence (*aretê*). It is a friend *who*—not *what*—helps me to live life more fully and not to feel cheated personally in the process.

Out of Isolation

Third, the growing trend toward mentors today may reflect the increasing isolation of the self within our society. Certainly people are awakening to the need of mentors as social dependence upon professions and institutions is weakening. Open, honest feedback is hard to obtain in the impersonal structures of society, where one's job may be at risk when there is too much personal vulnerability. Recognition, nurture, encouragement, attestation, and understanding—these are hard to find within a highly competitive, litigious, and politicized society such as ours. Also, when sexuality is adversarial, in a polarity of gender differences, again we become isolated, even within our gender differences. Mentoring as being "sexually complementary" may open more new horizons for us in our personal relationships than when we are only "politically correct."

To Walk the Talk

Fourth, in our day of tarnished leaders, fallen idols, and disenchanting heroes, we need moral exemplars who live as they talk, who integrate theory with practice, and whose unity of "head," "heart," and "arms" enables them to wholly make sense of their lives, public and private.[2]

Perhaps coming from broken homes, or broken marriages, or other experiences of dysfunctional relationships, people are looking to mentors to make "a difference" in their lives. It may be a fatherly or motherly presence, a loyal friend who treats us differently, someone who exemplifies what is true and wise counsel, or one who helps to provide stable relationships. For all these reasons, the presence of loving mentors as traveling companions on life's journey may open the prospect of the Promised Land indeed.

Starting in the 1950s, with the rise of the self-actualization movement and its cult of self-fulfillment, a cultural sea change began occurring. Already in 1966 Philip Rieff could speak of "the triumph of the therapeutic,"[3] meaning that Psychological Man had displaced Rational Man, with subjectivism displacing objectivism. New, paid "friendships" became available, with therapists hired specifically to "hear me" as my own family and friends had never "heard me" before, as long as the money lasted. Undoubtedly, the therapist has created an insatiable demand today for being heard by less expensive sympathizers. Perhaps the contemporary desire for mentors is thus also related to more awareness of differing forms of self-consciousness being experienced in place of conformities and conventional norms. These "life-worlds" we will critically explore.

In the business world, consultant services are analogous with institutionalized therapy, helping to restructure the ways business is organized. It is being called "shakedown." When leaders of industry need to make dramatic changes beyond the outside skills they may call upon, the inner support of wise friends still remains a vital need. So the cry is everywhere, "I need a mentor!"[4]

Functional Self-Identity

Perhaps most profoundly, the need today for mentors is, in light of the postmodern trend to redefine ourselves, no longer conventionally but inwardly so. We are not taking ourselves for granted as passively as in the past, either educationally, socially, sexually, or in other functions. Am I only a "thinking self" as the Aristotelian metaphysic has taught us to assume? Am I more than an "instrumental self," as Descartes has seduced us to think? Or am I merely the "doubting self," as followers of Nietzsche in their postmodern despair would tempt us to believe? All these various legacies have intensified a "functional" sense of self-identity today. But rebellious, reactionary choices of identity have become more possible than ever, all contributing to a new sense of the fragility of the self as it attempts to crate its own identity. More needful than ever before, we are asking our mentors—not Descartes's famous phrase, "I think therefore I am," but rather—"Is it okay for me to have the identity 'I-think-I-have'?" For surely nothing is more basic to myself than my identity for everything I do or desire to be in life!

Major Systems of Mentoring

Perhaps our analogy of the forest network of roots mentioned in the foreword does not go far enough. For we are also "environed." As fish swim in the sea and birds fly in the air, so human beings live within the historical and social environments of ideas, attitudes, and desires— shaped into forms of social consciousness inherited and further modified by us. That is to say, while we may individually be encouraged, reinforced, even inspired by other individuals, whose "roots" we may grow alongside as in a mentoring relationship, we are also conditioned socially by what the Germans call the *zeitgeist* or the "spirit of the age." These we may call "major systems of mentoring," or "metaethical systems," or even "life-situations" and "modes of consciousness."

The historical sweep of metaethical systems of mentoring that this book surveys is deliberately selective. It is not a historical survey. Rather it follows upon Søren Kierkegaard's three modes or levels of human existence: the Aesthetic, the Moral, and the Religious.

Heroic, Stoic, Therapeutic

In the first part of the book, we will look at the historic Heroic, Stoic, and Therapeutic models of mentoring. Briefly, the Heroic is a more bodily expression of consciousness, such as expressed in a warrior morality. The Stoic has a more deliberately moral code of behavior that is legislated and thought out intentionally. The Therapeutic has a more health-conscious behavior that involves individual as well as social health.

In researching these it struck me how close they are to Kierkegaard's three modes of consciousness or life-situations. However, they were developed independently before I began to pay attention to Kierkegaard's thought. This illustrates how a mentor can corroborate as well as guide us! Because these reflect on distinctive elements of our consciousness, they are more than passing historical models; they mark abiding influences that continue to intertwine and to distort the Christian interpretation of the self and of the wise mentoring needed.

It is significant that among theologians today there is a renaissance of Trinitarian scholarship. Interest in theological anthropology has risen, with a focus on persons, human and divine. Likewise, in the last three decades there has been renewed scholarly interest in studies on the thought of Kierkegaard. Curiously, the two movements have not been connected as they fruitfully could be. I have drawn upon both.

NEW WAYS OF COMMUNICATION

This book also implies that new ways of thinking will require new ways of communication. Mentoring has an indirectness of address that I shall try to cultivate in this text. It is *maieutic,* following the Socratic method of eliciting new ideas or insights from the other person. What is indirect and exemplary, rather than direct and informational, belongs to the more holistic communication among friends who care for each other. Thus, as we shall demonstrate in the following chapters, it is the eliciting *style* of the mentor, as well as the *content* of the message given, that communicates more effectively.

MENTORED BY GOD

The second half of the book describes how the Christian is mentored by faith in the personal character of the triune God, by His Word, and by prayer, for the ultimate purpose of worship. Thus we contrast the Western identity of the self-enclosure of the "individual" with the Christian understanding of the "person" as one who is "open to God." The person has also an eschatological orientation toward the "new" that God beckons us to enter into, of love and fellowship with Him and of our future destiny. For in this world, being an "individual" remains incomplete, leaving us with the restlessness that Augustine explored so deeply.

Implicit in the book is awareness of the modern distinction between sex and gender. Today "sex" denotes the biological difference of male and female, whereas since the 1970s, "gender" has become a psychosocial construct of differing emphases. *Sex polarity* has interpreted men and women differently from material bases, with a bias toward the superiority of the male, as in reaction some feminists now hold an inverse sexual polarity. Jacques Lacan has called the power games played by such polar attitudes "sexuation."[5] *Sex unity* is defined by philosophers who interpret sexual equality in intelligence, so their focus is in the realm of reason. *Sexual complement* rarely has been sustained in history other than in Christianity, for it is based upon the relational or personal dimension to which Christian faith gives unique understanding and interpretation.[6] It is this viewpoint that is also basic to this book. When Christians themselves have had a low view of personhood, often because of Aristotelian or Roman influences, then generally speaking they have also had a low or confused view of womanhood. Individualism and sexual polarity tend to belong together, because both have substantial or materialistic biases. Thus it is only in sexual complement that personhood can truly flourish.

Professional Christians versus "Friends of God"

The reader envisaged is the thoughtful Christian, perhaps one who is immersed in professional life and yet perceptive to see that a vital need today is to preserve the Christian life's "amateur status." For just as family life and friendship are where we live relationally, so is the Christian life. These are the realm of *dilettantes,* literally those taking "delight in" God, and as *amateurs* or "lovers" of each other. Our professional world scorns those in these categories as dabblers and unskilled hobbyists, which might suggest that Christian life cannot be taken with any seriousness in passionless professionalism!

Instead, however, of being awed and fascinated by the "professional way" of doing things, this book may help us rather to fear these distortions of Christian life as the contemporary cause for increasing unreality both of personal life and of faith. To reconsider and relive the Christian life as "befriended" in this homespun way is a passion behind this book. It is not written to advocate for a new mentoring market or a new program of theological education. Its purpose is to get to know oneself before God more simply and genuinely as a "friend of God," who treats us transparently as we really are!

Therefore, there cannot be any stereotype for our

unique identity before God. Every saint of God is a pattern, but no saint is *the* pattern. That is why we all need personal attention in discipleship and mentoring to guide us to "build our identity" righteously and socially to guard and guide us on our own journey of faith. This cannot ignore the Christian community or the vital role church life should have. Local churches are simply composed of members whose qualities of individuation, or their lack of it, will affect the whole community. Real persons are needed to contribute and give shape to real communities.

Individuals do not make communities, only persons. This, I will argue, is a theological rather than anthropological category. Persons, not merely individuals, mentored to be open to the Other, are receiving a new identity in the triune God of grace.

Part One

The Natural Individual

Ever seek to be the best and surpass all others in action.

—Homer

Between the ideal and the reality falls the shadow.

—T. S. Eliot

The Heroic Myth
of Mentor

Western civilization, with its Greek foundation, has ultimately been made possible by a belief in the special worth of human beings. The Greeks appraised humankind as unprecedented, as worthy of awe and wonder. Sophocles puts his inventions and enterprises in this perspective when he makes the chorus sing:

> There are many strange wonders, but nothing
> More wonderful than mankind.[1]

"See what a man I am, both strong and comely to look upon," says Achilles, while Protagoras declares, "Man is the measure of all things." This veneration of the uniqueness of man gave birth to the legends of mankind's association with the gods. For how else could man's use of speech, "of mind-swift thought," or the spirit to govern cities, or indeed man's first use of fire have arisen from the realm of the brute beasts alone? Likewise, man's upward struggle pointed to something beyond human nature. The Greeks assumed all these pointed to sources originally divine. Why then is man mortal, condemned to die, unlike the gods?

Here I interject: The emphasis and focus is on man; why not woman also? Homer, the presumed author of the *Iliad* who at least inspired the writing of the *Odyssey,* lived in the ninth or eighth century BC. He transformed oral tradition into sublime poetic diction, which expressed in new ways the experience of human emotions in their imaginary heroic encounters and exploits with gods and goddesses. This in turn led to a fascination with the human ability to think, so that the early Greek philosophers often interpreted the equality of the sexes in thought. However, Pythagoras (ca. 530 BC) was the first we know about who differentiated sexually the male virtue to rule and the female virtue to obey. Plato followed in recognizing sexual equality in intelligence, although Aristotle (424–347 BC) differed in creating a strong polarity between the sexes. However, in this earlier Homeric period that we are discussing in this chapter, what we will call the Heroic is strongly polarized around the male (a man's world indeed!).

The Pursuit of Excellence

Within the tragic ambiguity of man's godlike abilities and aspirations and yet his mortality, the Greeks distinguished between human education as *paideia,* or "child rearing," and *aretê,* or "excellence."[2] Every society trains its young by commandment and instruction in special skills appropriate to the two sexes. But cultural education fulfills a nobler purpose: it shapes the ideals for an elite within society, as *aretê* or excellence. *Aretê* indeed belongs to the gods, so that they or the *daimons* (geniuses) in their society were needed to nourish and to mentor it.

Thus Athena was the goddess of Athenian culture, as the wise centaur Chiron was for Achilles, hero of all heroes.[3] Homer himself was ascribed mentor of all tragic poets. He in turn had been mentored by Phoenix, his father's trusty servant. But while Achilles is heedless of his mentor's teachings, Telemachus, son of Odysseus (or in the Latin, Ulysses) is idealized as the docile pupil of his father's friend Mentes, the archetype of all mentors.

A Favored Few

This Greek tradition of the mentored life is thus elitist. For it is designed to shape the whole character of only the favored few—morally, intellectually, and socially. Its training is to cultivate a sense of duty (*aidos*), to exercise retributive justice (*nemesis*), and to give courage for single-handed combat in multiple adventures (*aristeia*).[4] Its intent is to represent godlikeness in ennobled self-interest, to remind lesser mortals of their divine origin. For surrounded by such role models, humankind is invited to imitate them as *paradeigma* (the origin of our word "paradigm").

This echoes the biblical teaching of human beings' unique creation in the image and likeness of God, although it is far from the self-revelatory character of God and of the reality of sin, as we shall see later. Yet it was on the ruins of this Greco-Roman world that Christendom arose, to lead to our contemporary religious confusion.[5]

THE HEROIC MYTH OF ODYSSEUS

We start, then, with Homer's *Odyssey* in the first of our studies of three historic models of mentoring. We will then contrast the Heroic model and its myth of Mentes with a Christian version.

A Greek hero of the Trojan Wars, Odysseus spends ten years in sea voyages to find his way home again from Troy to his native island of Ithaca (off the west coast of Greece). Some four centuries later, Aristotle in his *Poetics* gives us the essence of the plot of the story:

> A certain man has been abroad many years; he is
> alone, and the god of the sea Poseidon keeps a
> hostile eye on him. At home the situation is that
> suitors for his wife's hand are draining his
> resources and plotting to kill his son Telemachus.
> Then after suffering storm and shipwreck, he
> comes home, makes himself known, attacks the
> suitors: he survives and they are destroyed.[6]

Unmentioned by Aristotle is the fact that Odysseus is being constantly safeguarded by the shadowy presence of Athena. Meanwhile, "fatherless" Telemachus sets out to find his father, under the guardianship of Mentes.

Navigating against the primordial forces of the Mediterranean Sea becomes the main theater of this epic's actions. As T. S. Eliot observed about Mark Twain's tutelage, the acceptance of the River God was vital to his adolescent development, for "it is the subjection of Man that gives to Man his dignity. For without some kind of God, Man is not even very interesting."[7] While the river may symbolize the self as "sullen, untamed, intractable," observed Walt Whitman, the sea is the vast dimension of the chaotic and eternal. Man's dignity is to pit himself against unfathomable forces that would thus both create and challenge his meaningful existence. As a schoolboy, James Joyce already had decided Ulysses was his favorite hero, and so years later he chose him for the prototype of his own major work, the novel *Ulysses*.[8] Hermann Hesse in *Demian* and other novels does the same thing, defining what he means by heroic as "only that individual can be heroic who takes his own meaning" from his own natural willfulness as his fate.[9]

VOYAGE OF EVERYMAN

Many have interpreted the voyage of Odysseus, in which so many perils and hardships had to be overcome, as an intimation of Everyman's voyage through life. It is a voyage beset with many deadly perils and temptations, and yet it is capable of such glorious achievements. Escape, enlightenment, the caresses of goddesses, honor, fame, war, and victory all seem to ennoble Man, archetypically so.[10] But the journey is really within, whether in Odysseus or the archetype, while the stopping places represent his particular psychological conditions and problems, and the goddesses his own sexual desires and fantasies. The restless "fabulous voyager," in reality, is neurotic. So Odysseus's "return home" to accept his mortality is actually the time when he is restored to his own personal consciousness, to domestic reality, and to family responsibility.[11] There, ironically, he faces more real dangers than all the time he was abroad! The fantasy of Odysseus thus deepens the yearning question of the popular song of two generations ago: "What's It All About, Alfie?" Is it not all about finding out who you really are?

In the third century, Clement of Alexandria is quite sure of his response to such a question. He contrasts the pagan Odysseus with the Christian, for in spite of all Odysseus's famous exploits, he and such heroes "care little about life eternal, for like the ancient from Ithaca they do not hunger for the truth or for their heavenly homeland, but only for the smoke of their earthly homes."[12] This is echoed in Homer's own description of Odysseus:

> Straining for no more than a glimpse of hearth-smoke drifting up from his own land, Odysseus longs to die …

Meanwhile, Odysseus's wife, Penelope, waits twenty long years at home, bereft of her husband:

> Odysseus—if he could return to tend my life the renown I had would only grow in glory. Now my life is a torment.[13]

"Self-Fulfillment"

The high value placed upon a single person with his or her own aesthetic notion of what is due him or her is not unlike the contemporary cult of "leadership." It is the self-asserting principle that seeks honor through the senses in visible action. Even in the more contemplative posture of the later Greek philosophers, there was still the pursuit of knowledge for its own sake. Just as we pursue "excellence" today, so from early times the Greeks valued *aretê* as the full utilization of humankind's inborn capacities. It was what is now narcissistically called "self-fulfillment."

Moreover, because of their kinship with the gods, and by the readiness of the gods to inspire and direct them, the Greeks had deep appreciation for the potentials humans could exhibit. However, morality set limitations to desired capacities. Eventually, what mattered was that the hero utilized his potentials fully, regardless of others. Conflict with others and the test to conquer others intensified the instinct of self-preservation and self-aggrandizement. Such then is Odysseus as a "great storyteller" of the self:

> Given hospitality by Aretê, Queen of the
> Phaeacians never faltering, filling with winning
> self-control, he shines forth at assembly grounds
> and people gaze at him like a god when he walks
> through the streets.[14]

When I left the security and status of Oxford University, with its strong classical tradition of this Heroic idealism, a colleague gave me a book just published called *The Ulysses Factor*.[15] My friend could only interpret my midlife decision to go out into the unknown with no tangible prospects as a quest to be challenged by something, accept it, and rise above it. For some, this thing is to climb the highest mountains, to sail the oceans single-handedly, to create Olympic sports for the disabled, or whatever gives the plain challenge that it is "there to be done," or "to be discovered," or "to be found out."

So too Homer wrote his two poems, the *Iliad* and the *Odyssey*, to communicate how the chaotic forces of war and water are there to be overcome by human courage. The universality of Odysseus has appealed to our greatest poets and dramatists: Virgil, Ovid, Dante, Calderon, Shakespeare, Milton, Tennyson, Joyce, Eliot, and others. Odysseus can wander years in the realms of fantasy or even live out all his emotions within twenty-four hours in the streets of Dublin, as in Joyce's novel *Ulysses*. We can identify with his emotions anywhere.

Individualism and Narcissism

The essence of this Heroic outlook, whether it be held by Odysseus or Columbus or James Bond or even *Esquire* magazine, is what fosters individualism and narcissism. It powers the self-endowed prowess of the adventurer; the restless questioner with an enlarged sense of self-confidence; the strong personality; the public persona; the sculpted, artistic exhibitionist for all to see and admire.

In the strongly visual heritage of Greek sculpture, the gods are the custodians of human morality, fickle and humanlike as their passions may be. As archetypes, they invite us to interpret human existence not as meaningless, but as a metaphysical backdrop for the human drama. But the intermixture of natural and supernatural, human initiative and the fates, does create ambiguities. Is it the wayward wrath of the sea-god Poseidon that drives Odysseus off course in his sea voyages, or is it his own waywardness? Are they the goddesses Calypso or Circe who would entice him, or his own sexual fantasies?

Tennyson said Ulysses was not so much driven by the deities as by his own senses. Jungian therapists today make this double interpretation of archetypes for our own "personalities" a less serious burden than naked self-centeredness. But ultimately the hero is left to himself, to know for himself, to experience for himself, to will for himself, in a self-controlling inner universe of willfulness and pride. He is equipped for all this in courage, selfishness, practical competence, physical strength, powerful imagination, ability to lead, self-discipline, self-endurance, self-sufficiency, unscrupulousness, and strong sexual attractions. But all confound the restlessness of his own soul. As Tennyson tells us:

I cannot rest from travel: I will drink
Life to the lees: all times I have enjoy'd
Greatly, have suffer'd greatly, both with those
That loved me and alone; on shore, and when
Thro' scudding drifts the rainy Hyades
Vext the dim sea: I am become a name;
For always roaming with a hungry heart
Much have I seen and known; cities of men
And manners, climates, councils, governments.
My self not least but honour'd of them all;
And drunk delight of battle with my peers.
Far on the ringing plains of windy Troy.
I am a part of all that I have met;
Yet all experience is an arch wherethro'
Gleams that untravell'd world, whose margin fades
For ever and for ever when I move.[16]

Yet Odysseus too is mortal, and as the years increase, he has to admit his declining powers:

Tho' much is taken, much abides, and tho'
We are not now that strength which in old
     days
Moved earth and heaven; that which we are,
     we are
One equal temper of heroic hearts.
Made weak by time and fate, but strong in will
     to strive, to seek, to find, and not to yield.[17]

The advantage of myth is that it is flexible to our own perspectives, to our whims and the psyche of our own temperaments. For it is symbolic of deep and mysterious levels of our existence. Myth is therefore also comprehensive of the human condition, so that while the shape of the myths may change with culture, their virility endures.

Odysseus in Modern Culture

Odysseus lives on in our secular society; we know him well. For perhaps he mirrors ourselves; indeed he is a part of you and me. His traits are indelibly human and therefore natural to us. However, modern Odysseus is, by his own myth making, fragmented, self-ignorant, and unreal, for he lives only by the senses. He has to live several roles at the same time. The recent obituary of a celebrity noted that the famous man could never imagine not living with a wife and several mistresses at the same time. Throughout his life, this celebrity had functioned with several compartments and personae, all separated from each other. With the loss of a center, the soulless soul that sensualizes everything can only make an empty "personality" into a series of masquerades through life, as Odysseus did. He can never get life all together, within one heart and one mind. Life can never be simple and uncomplicated. This is the tragedy of so many today!

Also, as in our culture, the Homeric world is not one in which women can expect fair play, and certainly not sexual complementarity. Penelope, the wife of Odysseus, is left abandoned for twenty years, so she has to use every feminine trick to defend herself from her suitors, like the stereotype of the Australian manipulative "sheila" depicted today. Male comradeship is for public self-interest. Home life is obscure, while tenderness must be hidden.[18]

The Myth of Mentor

Humankind, though, cannot dwell only with its own irrational sinfulness and desires. So the Greeks appreciated the need of a world order, of a rationale for life and culture. Hence, the mentor plays this vital role of helping others to make sense of their lives, especially men.

Telemachus, Odysseus's young son, is left to the charge of his old friend Mentes with these instructions: "I leave with you this son, whom I so tenderly love; watch over his infancy if you have love of me, keep flattery far from him; teach him to vanquish his passions." Thus Telemachus represents the docile, undramatic, even non-Greek type of individual that is still despised today. Greek *aretê* is essentially "to take possession of the beautiful," or "the glamorous" today, in an intensely developed, yet momentary, self-love. Even Aristotle later admits,

> For such a man [that is, a Heroic one] would prefer short intense pleasures to long quiet ones; would choose to live nobly for a year rather than to pass many years of ordinary life; would rather do one great and noble deed than many small ones.[19]

Thus the mentored life dwells unpopular beneath the shadows of this dramatic and Heroic lust for life. The docile life is not dramatic enough; it does not face the tragedy faced by the self-willfulness of Odysseus or others like Achilles. Yet the Greek tension is that, nevertheless, it is wise to be nurtured by the gentle Mentes. We too recognize the folly of living in a fatherless society (although our culture of divorce is but an expression of the Heroic values we stubbornly want to enjoy. Our own world wars—like Troy's—have upset the traditional values of the hearth and of motherly nurture). Like Homer we know that the loss of the hearth is the loss of reality.

Another point resonates with our modern psychology. In spite of having Mentes with him as a surrogate father, the inherited character of Telemachus has not changed. So during the search for his father, Telemachus finds himself caught up in the same temptations, enamored by the same goddesses as his father, to demonstrate the adage "like father, like son." The parental hypocrisy persists—for Mentes is requested to guard Telemachus, despite the fact that Odysseus never guarded his son himself. The son of the absentee husband in turn has the concerns to protect his own mother, as she had never been protected maritally—a dysfunctional family indeed! Yet each is too involved in "finding oneself" to experience a wholesome family life.[20] For the Greeks, ideally, the family was a unit that was older than the state, and whose priority did in theory come first. But ambition, violence, and self-glorification really had priority, not the family.

THE CHRISTIAN FABLE OF TELEMACHUS

The myth of Odysseus or Ulysses is well-known in Western literature. The only systematic use made of the myth of Mentor has been in the novel *Les Aventures de Télémaque* (*The Adventures of Telemachus*), written in 1699 by François Fénelon (1651–1715).[21] A series of pedagogical essays, it is a fable of high moral seriousness.

Fénelon was the younger son of a Gascon nobleman. Mentored by Jean-Jacques Olier (1608–1657) and his pupil Tronson, Fénelon was inspired by them to live a life of obscurity and not to enter the race for social preferment and external recognition. This is how he cultivated his inner assurance and personal authority within the abiding presence of Christ. Thus he could be indifferent and therefore independent in heart from the external authority of court life.

Nevertheless, Fénelon was tutor to the Duke of Burgundy, eldest grandson of King Louis XIV and heir to the French throne, from age six to fourteen years old

(1689–1697). As such, Fénelon had a tough and dangerous task to perform. The duke was an *enfant terrible.*
Saint-Simon observed, "He was so impetuous as to
desire to break the clocks when they struck the hour
summoning him to do something he did not like, and
fell into the most extraordinary fury against the rain
when it interfered with his desires. Opposition threw
him into a passion."[22] In other words, he was a child
autocrat like his grandfather, another Ulyssean figure.
Yet by the time Fénelon had completed his mentoring
duties eight years later, the duke had become gentle,
patient, wise beyond his fourteen years, and Fénelon's
friend for life.

Sadly for both, however, the moral example of
Fénelon's character showed up antithetically against
Louis XIV's vices. The king's jealousy and insecurity
were inflamed into anger against Fénelon by evil-
minded courtiers, and he forbade pupil and mentor to
ever see each other again. Yet, a secret correspondence
carried on between Fénelon and the duke revealed the
mutual love and loyalty that bound them ever closer to
one another for the rest of their lives.

Included in the correspondence were fables Fénelon
had written for the duke based on the imagined wan-
derings of Telemachus in search of his father in the
companionship of Mentor. To expose Fénelon to the
king's displeasure and without Fénelon's knowledge,
The Adventures of Telemachus was stolen and published.
This could not have come at a worse time for Fénelon.
He had already been driven from the court with his
appointment as archbishop of Cambrai on the north-
ern frontier of the country. Louis XIV read into
Telemachus an indictment of his own autocratic rule,
and he judged Fénelon to be a critical and disloyal subject. In vain, Fénelon attempted to defend himself as

being "anti-heroic" in his mentoring of the duke, without being disloyal to his king:

> I should have shown myself to be not only one of the most ungrateful but the most reckless of men if I had attempted to take satirical and insolent examples; I shrunk from the very thought of such a thing. Certainly in the *Adventures* I have set forth the essential truths and pitfalls of a sovereign power, but I have not emphasized any so as to point to any individual character. The more you read the book, the more you will see that I wished to be outspoken without being personal. Moreover this published version is not the same as the original.[23]

Ironically, Fénelon's position had been made possible by the esteem of a lady at the court, the Duchess de Beauvilliers. She was the daughter of Jean-Baptiste Colbert, the king's minister of finance, and her husband was controller of the Dauphine's household. A young Fénelon had written a first educational treatise, *De l'éEducation des filles,* to assist in her eight daughters' education. That led to his selection to this highly competitive post to shape and mentor the future king of France! Throughout his life, it was the power of empathy, of entering into the difficulties and feelings of others, and of realizing temptations that gave him the emotional and moral intelligence that he also exercised toward the young prince.

A Book Influential and Misunderstood

As spiteful as the publication of Fénelon's *Telemachus* had been, it became one of the most popular books in print during the next two centuries. It was widely interpreted in the revolutionary climate of France and North

America as intolerant of patriarchy and cause for the rejection of the monarchy; and so, in the climate of revolt, it was considered to be a great political revolutionary statement. Inspired by it, Voltaire wrote *Candide,* and Rousseau wrote *Emile.*[24]

However, whereas Fénelon had composed a fable of Christian instruction (in German, *Erziehungroman*), these Enlightenment writers only introduced a new type of novel for secular education (*Bildungsroman*).[25] Fénelon's work was more reflective of an extrinsic, hierarchical ordering of life—God, king, and then other authorities. In the new secular approach, authority was intrinsic to oneself. One's life was held in only by happenstance, with free associations focused upon individual choices and achievements. Later, Charles Dickens' novel *David Copperfield* becomes exemplary of this new genre, where, without a mentor, the solitary hero faces the new perplexities of urbanized society, now all in flux. Survival, not social ascription, opens up a new realm of social mobility and its destiny. It is also a world of shifting moral values, which are in sharp contrast to the fixed universe and unimpeachable instructions of the authoritarian *ancien régime.*

It is thus one of the ironies of literary history to have Fénelon attributed as a pioneer in this new genre when secularists cannot hear his Christian voice. They think they are hearing the voice of a political revolutionary. It is, in fact, the prophetic voice of a Christian reformer—and not as a Protestant but as a Catholic.

So while he accepts the myth of Telemachus and makes a good story out of it to amuse and educate a young wayward prince into the ways of truth, Fénelon is really a Christian fabulist. To be accepted and praised for the very things he was trying to condemn is irony indeed! Political ambition was the last thing he wanted, even at the French court. His old friend Cardinal Bossuet turned against him in jealousy and interpreted him as a cunning strategist, as indeed Bossuet was himself. Fénelon, along with his soul friend Madame Guyon, suffered character assassination. Later, intellectuals were to reinterpret *The Adventures of Telemachus* both as political satire and as a new manifesto for educational development—never understanding his Christian motives. To a Christian mentor like Fénelon, his retelling of Telemachus was incompatible with Homer, or indeed with the king of France. So who was he? How was he like the mythical Mentes?

FÉNELON AS A CHRISTIAN MENTOR

In response to the advancement of his pupil to the life of the court, Father Tronson wrote to Fénelon:

> You are in a land where the Gospel of Jesus Christ is little known, when those who know it make use of it for personal advancement. You now live among people whose conversation is practically pagan, whose example tends to dangerous things. You will find yourself surrounded by everything calculated to indulge in the senses and awaken dormant desires ... in truth you are in a dangerous position; it must be candidly acknowledged that it will be difficult to remain steadfast in it, that you need the highest principles to sustain you. If ever you needed study and meditation on the Bible it is now; until now you have looked to it to strengthen you with the truth, and inspire you with good thoughts; now you will need to banish evil ones and shield you from lies.... You will perhaps esteem my letter ... a misplaced sermon rather than an apt congratulation. I should be more brief and less outspoken if I were not too eager for your welfare.[26]

Thus was the mentor of the young prince mentored!

How well Fénelon learned from such a faithful Christian mentor can be gauged later by the ways Fénelon himself learned to write his *Letters of Spiritual Counsel* to those Ulyssean personalities who needed radical transformation—both men and women, for Fénelon lived comfortably with sexual complementarity. Part of the enduring power of these letters is their highly personal character, whereas the Homeric poems are written for Everyman. Moreover, Fénelon was not intent on literary acclaim, but on comforting, counseling, and directing specifically the hearts of those who confided so intimately with him. Fénelon replies to one such correspondent: "Listen in quietness and silence for what God asks of you, and then do only that. You will see that all that is excessive will restrain itself and all that is insufficient will teach you the right medium."[27]

As Tronson had often been blunt with Fénelon, so Fénelon in turn is also transparently honest and open in his approach to his confidantes. He needed no platitudes, threadbare in their repetition, to cover the truths that were his guide to godly living. The practice of confession should lead to such openness, so on one occasion, Fénelon wrote: "You must confess everything with simplicity, however much it costs you."[28]

Fénelon, equally at ease in mentoring men or women, wrote to one proud lady-in-waiting at court:

> Let me show you, my dear daughter, what it seems to me that God desires I should lay before you. The mainstay that you have unconsciously cherished in your heart since childhood is immoderate self-esteem, hidden beneath the semblance of sensibility and heroic generosity—love of the fantastic, the fallacy of which no one has ever revealed to you.[29]

He could not have struck Odysseus himself a more mortal blow against pride! He then went on to show her that actually this weakness related also to her overscrupulous nature, as well as to her apparent generosity: "All your care proceeds from the fear of not being sufficiently pleased with yourself: this is the secret of your scruples. You wish that God as well as man should be pleased with you, and that you should be pleased with yourself in all that you do."[30]

Such letters must have been painful reading to their recipients. Yet Fénelon is ready and able to expose himself no less ruthlessly: "I am covered with mire and I feel that I sin perpetually because I am not guided by the Spirit. The sense of my own eminence excites me.... I am ... fundamentally devoted to myself. Finally, I cannot understand my real self."[31] So he sees himself as an "unworthy instrument" on behalf of others. From the mutuality of mentor and mentored as sinners before God, Fénelon could thus write:

> Put aside all pride of intellect and soaring speculations: open your heart to Him and tell Him everything. Then having done so, listen to His voice. You should have so prepared yourself that your whole being waits silent for His utterance that your heart lie open to the impress of His wishes. This silence of our being, suspending our earthly passions, our human thoughts, is absolutely essential if we would hear the Voice which summons us to the entire sacrifice to self, to worship God in spirit and in truth.[32]

The essence then of Fénelon's spirituality is summed up in another letter of counsel, which he wrote shortly before he died:

Anxiety and misgiving proceed solely from love of self. The love of God accomplishes all things quietly and completely: it is not anxious nor uncertain. The Spirit of God rests continually in quietness. "Perfect love casts out fear." It is in forgetfulness of self that we find peace. Wherever self comes in it inflames our hearts, and for its subtle poison there is no antidote. Happy is he who yields himself, completely, finally, and unconsciously.[33]

Then he adds: "I pray that God Himself will speak to you, and that you will follow faithfully what He says to you. Listen to the inward whisper of His Spirit and follow it—that is enough; but to listen one must be silent, and to follow one must yield." Thus did Fénelon care more for the truth than for other people's good opinion of him. "Disinterested love should make us disinterested in all our opinions, impartial in our views, I wish nothing for my own," Fénelon confessed to a fellow priest.[34]

Purity of Heart

Perhaps what Fénelon gained most of all from the unrighteousness inflicted upon him was a deepened humility before God, as well as uncomplaining submissiveness to the powers that sought to destroy him. He showed a purity of heart and saintliness that was unimpeachable despite all the efforts of his enemies. He learned personally that "the best things become the most polluted, because abuse of them is worse than the abuse of that which is less good." Such was his reply to those who upheld the system of spiritual direction, which was being abused within the church at that time. His response was not to abolish it but to redeem it in good hands. "I ask nothing better than to help you," was the keynote of his position. For he knew how to encourage the doubters, to bring hope to the sorrowful, and to set a counsel of maturity before those who were godly. But all this required the absolute sacrifice of the self, something he strove for but never thought he had yet reached, nor came near reaching in himself.

Fénelon's own selflessness is surely a vital key to his success in being such an effective spiritual mentor to others. He interpreted this essential need of selflessness, saying:

> The first of God's gifts, the foundation of all others, is which I call self. He gave me myself. To Him I owe not only all I have, but all I am ... the mind of Man can now understand the infinity of such a gift. The God Who made me, gave me myself, the self I love so much I owe to His goodness, and God should be in me and I in Him, seeing I derive myself from Him. Without Him I should not be myself, without Him I should not have the self I love nor the power of loving it, neither the will to love nor the thoughts whereby I know myself. All that I have and am is given me.[35]

Nothing could be more anti-Ulyssean in spirit than the Christian spirit of Fénelon, nor could Telemachus have had a more contrasted mentor than Fénelon was to the friends he cherished. He declared:

> We shall find peace, not in subtle arguments, but in the simplicity of prayer; not in abstract speculations but in daily practical morality; not in listening to, but in silencing ourselves; not in flattering ourselves that we fathom the designs of

> God, but in accepting perpetual ignorance of
> them, content to love Him, regardless of the
> uncertainty of a salvation towards which we never
> cease to yearn. For to die daily will rob our final
> death of all its sharpness.[36]

He died with the thoughts of 2 Corinthians 4:16; 5:9 before him: "We do not lose heart. Though outwardly we are wasting away, yet inwardly we are being renewed day by day.... So we make it our goal to please him, whether we are at home in the body or away from it."

THE OBSESSION WITH ODYSSEUS CONTINUES

Odysseus's adventures still have hold upon our imagination, for fascination with the carnal life of the body has never changed. It is as the apostle Paul expresses it to be: "the lust of the flesh, and the lust of the eyes, and the pride of life."[37] Obsession with the appearance and the prowess of the body are more exaggerated than ever, while heroes as fashion models or sports idols are prominent in our daily news. One writer speaks of late adulthood as the period of great potential. It's a time for the "Ulyssean adult," when career changes, possibly marital changes, and all the maturation of self-actualization have fully developed. This is still based upon all that the Greeks believed in: "man the measure of all things" (Protagoras); "nothing is more wonderful than man ... speech too, and wind-swift thought, he has taught himself" (Sophocles); "see what a man I am, both strongly and comely to look upon" (Homer).[38]

There is, I assure you, a medical art for the soul. It is philosophy, whose aid need not be sought, as in bodily diseases, from outside ourselves.... We must endeavor with all resources and all our strength to become capable of doctoring ourselves.[1]

—Cicero

Stoicism is the refuge for the individual in an indifferent or hostile world too big for him; it is the permanent substratum of a number of versions of cheering oneself up.... The Stoical attitude is the reverse of Christian humility.[2]

—T. S. Eliot

THE STOIC AS THE MORAL MENTOR

Cicero's and Eliot's interpretations of Stoicism are separated by two millennia. As such, they reflect upon the remarkable longevity and persistent influence the metaethical mentoring system known as Stoicism has had within our Western culture.

When the apostle Paul encountered both Epicurean and Stoic philosophers in the agora of Athens, the Epicureans dismissed his teaching, while the Stoics were more open to it (see Acts 17:17–21). Paul used a Stoic diction in parts of his speech, quoting their poet Aratus that echoed the didactic of Cleanthes' hymn to Zeus. The rational nature of the cosmos; the autonomy of conscience; the higher authority of divinity as the voice of God within the conscience; the role of asceticism in curbing the passions; and the moral demands for exemplars were all Stoic elements of morality that Christian thinkers again and again throughout history have associated with Christianity. Even the Reformers, imbued with humanism, gave approval to Stoic morals. Indeed, Christendom has imbibed no other extraneous influence more deeply, especially when the biblical doctrine of sin is overlooked, that is, in the human usurpation of the role and sphere of God.

While the Ulyssean or Odyssean model remained competitive and localized as a warrior mentality for individual achievement, the development of Greek civilized urbanity, especially that of the later Hellenistic empire, demanded new scales of morality. Stoicism provided this in interpreting the whole cosmos as being intrinsically rational and humans being innately rational, enabling them to interpret their own emotions and actions within its sphere.

The Stoic ideal of the human being as the "citizen of the world" thus became a moral system appropriate for the vastness of the Roman Empire and even beyond.[3] Well-being, or *eudaimonia,* was interpreted as the right activity of reason, with a strong sense of self-teaching.

The Greeks had first selected the "cardinal virtues" as pivotal to the "good life" from astrological origins, identifying them as prudence, fortitude, justice, and temperance with the influences of the four planets. They were called cardinal because they hinged (hinge is *cardo* in Greek) and interlocked logically with each other. Later Aristotle (384–322 BC) could give his son Nichomachus a rational justification for "the virtuous life," as it came to be known. Yet he did not believe women could be included in that life. For him "justice" was the premier virtue, enabling only male citizens to enjoy "the good life," or *bios,* of civic affairs. Plato (ca. 428–348 BC), accepting sexual equality, argued plausibly that a woman's virtue lay in managing her household, as a man might be engaged in civic affairs. Both philosophers had a blind spot about slaves and barbarians, for whom the virtuous life was not applicable.

Stoicism, however, was much more universal, accepting the equality of women as well as contrasting the rationality of all mankind with the instinct of animals.[4]

THE ASSUMPTIONS OF STOICISM

The founding father of Stoicism, Zeno (ca. 333–261 BC) came to Athens ten years after Aristotle's death, so Stoicism grew contiguously with much of the great Greek philosophers' teachings. Leadership of the Stoics' school passed on to Cleanthes (d. 231 or 232 BC), and then to Chrysippus (ca. 282–206 BC). The Stoics developed several basic assumptions:

- The whole world is a simple organic unity, material in nature. Within it every event is linked causally with every other event, so reality is rational, enclosed, and material. None of the gods in this polytheistic system is transcendent, although Zeus is the agent of periodic fire that causes the earth to perish (the doctrine of *ekpyrosis*). *Pneuma* is the vitalizing creative principle, but it is also material, while the *Logos* structures reality and determines human knowledge.[5]
- Man has the faculty of reason to be able to reenact the world within his own mind.
- While animals have only a basic instinct for self-preservation, humanity has the moral impulse to be oneself, or *oikeiosis*, living according to one's own nature and condition. Three steps are involved in this Stoic concept of *oikeiosis:*[6] (1) being self-conscious; (2) having a natural love of self; and (3) being attached to oneself.[7]
- By the time of Cicero (106–43 BC), virtue itself had become interpreted as the fruit of rational inquiry—a shift from being merely virtuous to being right about it![8] Now, in a much more materialistic universe, no

longer populated by *daimons* or spirits, human actions were interpreted as being "up to us." To have reason was now believed to be a fully human attribute. So Cicero now denied that "a happy spirit," or *eudaimonia,* was the primary value that the Greeks had believed in. Rather, it was having "cognition" of the cosmic law.[9]

- Writing to Lucilius, Seneca (ca. 1–65) takes a step further, saying, "It is stupid to pray [that is, to have a good understanding] [for] the god is near you, with you, inside you … a holy spirit is seated within us, a watcher and guardian of our good and bad actions. As this spirit is treated by us, so it treats us."[10] Like adherents of the New Age today, the claim is made that we have divinity within ourselves.[11]

Passions and Apatheia

Because of the emphasis on the rational development of the moral life, it has been assumed the Stoics had a highly disparaging view of the human emotions. Rather, they wanted reason to *control* one's emotional responses. They put philosophy to therapeutic use to eliminate passion, which they defined as pleasure and pain (in the present condition) and desire and fear (in the future). Then one could cultivate self-sufficiency like a virtuous god.

As a good doctor, the wise Stoic mentor should advise each individual appropriately, focusing upon the specific situation that may have upset the patient-pupil. Personal narrative is important to examine, then, to suggest the right rational strategy to adopt. Always the objective is to take charge of one's own education, even to learn self-teaching. Poetry may give significant help here, although it should be used with caution among young persons, argues Plutarch.[12]

The passions, however, will always continue to

threaten self-control. Because they cannot be eradicated altogether, at least analyze them! Those Stoics who were more medically curious gave more attention to the emotions. Posidonius (ca. 135–50 BC) argued that the passions do exist, and a nonrational explanation of them was appropriate. Galen (129–199), also a physician, contributed to the notion of "excess" that may dominate and take over one's more balanced, rational thought to create tensions.[13] The body requires symmetry for health, so why not also for the psyche (soul)?

The Stoic concept of *apatheia,* detachment from the passions, was the idealized ability of maintaining a rationalized worldview. Passions were judged accordingly as intemperate, unbalanced, or inconsistent with reason and prudence. Thus for the Stoics, the basic virtue was not valor, as it was for Homer, nor justice, as it was for Aristotle. It was temperance, in the sense of control of the emotions.

Transcending Circumstances

Seneca, mentor of Nero and a contemporary of Paul the apostle, argued that distinction should be given to two kinds of passion: that which was rash and hasty and that which was weak-willed. A diplomatic Stoic with experienced courtly wisdom,[14] Seneca taught that neither kind reflected a considered view that required time and perspective to help people distance themselves from false passions, to gain *apatheia.* For example, the cure for such a passion as mourning was to learn how to reinterpret one's loss or pain differently from before. Perhaps one was too attached to the loved one now gone or to the pleasure lost.[15]

Thus the more sophisticated Stoicism of Cicero and later especially of Seneca was to know how to mentor distinctly in each circumstance and with each individual, rather like the mental strategies now adopted by cognitive therapy. By such means, "magnanimity" might be achieved, not in the revised meaning of forgiveness, but in the original meaning of having mental transcendence over one's circumstances. Indeed, in late Stoicism, magnanimity became considered the crown of the virtues.

STOICISM AND PAUL THE APOSTLE[16]

Paul, growing up as Saul in Tarsus—a great educational center of Stoicism—also claimed a magnanimous spirit. "For I have learned to be content whatever the circumstances.... I have learned the secret of being content in any and every situation." However, the source of his magnanimity was wholly incompatible with self-grounded Stoicism. His life was "in Christ," not in himself: "I can do everything through him who gives me strength."[17] Likewise, *apatheia* for Paul does not mean standing alone and detached; rather "godliness with contentment is great gain," he assured Timothy.[18] Thus, Christianity, as expressed by Paul, confronts and challenges Stoicism.

Paul's Encounter with Stoicism

Paul's address on Mars Hill is the only biblical reference naming the Epicureans and Stoics (see Acts 17:18). The Epicureans were opposed to popular religious superstitions, but they were condemned for their disbelief in providence and divine revelation—perhaps theirs was "the unknown god" the apostle refers to in his address. The Stoics, on the other hand, Paul commended for their desire to believe in providence and for their belief in the equality of all people. But their worship was of "nature rather than of Nature's God." It has been suggested that it was concerns raised by Posidonius[19] that Paul was responding to, as well as in quoting from the Stoic poet Aratus.

Perhaps the central issue the former Saul of Tarsus encountered as he was surrounded by Stoics in his own boyhood education was "how can the wise man live in accordance with nature?" After his conversion, Paul makes the "natural man" his target in writing to the Corinthians. Quoting from Isaiah 29:14, Paul speaks in condemnation of the Stoic as a self-grounded self: "I will destroy the wisdom of the wise, and the cleverness of the clever I will thwart."[20]

Stoic Autonomy

The Stoic is self-contained (*oikeiosis*), whereas God has called us to be "in Christ," to be a new creation no longer self-grounded "in the flesh." A person renewed by the Spirit of God is no longer *psychikos,* or natural humanity, but *pneumatikos,* or spiritual man or woman. The former is impotent to change humankind, for it exists in a condition of enmity toward God.[21] Blind and unaware of God, the Stoic cannot conceive of "sin," for it is only by theological insight that the sinful condition can have any real meaning. This debate, then, between Paul and the Stoics rings very contemporary, because our culture is still so permeated by the similar spirit of autonomy.

This ongoing debate is well illustrated by Paul's letter to the Philippians. He begins his letter desirous that his converts will be "filled with the fruit of righteousness that comes through Jesus Christ" (1:11), a flat contradiction of the Stoic recipe for the virtuous life. He even makes mention of the word *aretê*[22] as the Stoics used it for moral excellence, but in the context of heart and mind guarded in Christ Jesus (4:7). Paul, like his Lord as described in the gospel of Matthew, does not believe in some abstract qualities of "the Good," as the Stoics did.[23] Rather, his list of good qualities are varied to the circumstances and are the fruit of God's Spirit, not of the human spirit. So Paul gives no ethical treatise, but always particularizes the contents and context of his admonitions.[24] God, in Christ, by His Spirit, is the source and character of true virtue.

As Paul has so modeled his life "in Christ," so he would encourage others, such as the Philippians, to imitate him (2:2). The model displayed by Christ is much before him as he writes to the Philippians, saying, "Being confident of this, that he who began a good work in you will carry it on to completion until the day of Christ Jesus" (1:6).

Moral Self-Sufficiency

Stoicism's view of virtue is that it reflects moral self-sufficiency for its own sake and extirpates the passions. Therefore it can be rationally controlled and effected deliberately by self-disciplined effort. This virtuous life, argued Musonius Rufus (ca. 30–101), a more modest Stoic philosopher than most, is now in a unique role human beings can live to reflect and resemble God. Writing to Epictetus, Rufus said:

> We can imagine nothing even in gods better than prudence, justice, courage, and temperance. Therefore as God through the possession of these virtues is unconquered by pleasure or greed; is superior to desire, envy, and jealousy; is high-minded, beneficent, and kindly ... so also human kind is the image of Him, when living in accord with nature should be thought of as being like Him.[25]

But for Paul, the revelation of God is in the God-man, Jesus Christ, in whom all Christians are united within the fellowship of His Spirit. This is not because they share in the same virtues and by them move themselves up to Him. It is because He has descended to be human, in humiliation and self-emptying: "Who, being in very nature God, did not consider equality with God something to be grasped, but made himself nothing," indeed to take the form of a man.[26]

So as He is the humble God, so humility is the basic attitude of His followers, an attitude inconceivable to the Stoics. All true life for the Christian flows from the death and resurrection of Christ, foolishness indeed to the self-achieving Greeks. Whereas ethics is self-contained for the Stoic, ethics and theology are inseparable for the Christian. It is God's own character and nature that prescribe true human nature and purpose, not the "pursuit of excellence" for its own sake.[27]

A Therapeutic versus a Redeemed Community

The cultivation of a harmonious personality, constant serenity, and balance in mental health are eulogized, however, by Seneca, as secular therapists still do:

> I shall tell you what I mean by health: if the mind is content with its own self; if it has confidence in itself; if it understands that all those things for which men pray, all the benefits which are bestowed and sought for, are of no importance in relation to a life of happiness; under such conditions it is sound. The effect of wisdom is a joy that is unbroken and continuous. The mind of the wise is like the ultra-lunar firmament; eternal calm pervades that region, it is consistent with itself throughout.[28]

This Stoic joy is further defined in a letter Seneca wrote to his young friend Lucilius: "Take joy only in that which comes from what is your own. What do I mean by *what is your own*? I mean you yourself and your own best part."[29]

Paul, however, who speaks relationally of joy sixteen times in the epistle to the Philippians, indeed has a very different interpretation.[30] His is never solitary, always social joy. He always prays to God with joy (1:4). He "joys" in the progress of others in the Christian faith (1:25). Joy is a communal emotion that gives coherence to the Philippian community, for it is shared. The Philippians were not to look to their own interests (as in *oikeiosis*) but rather to those of others (2:4). Indeed, the whole purpose of the epistle is an illustration of the social character of Christian mentoring as beneficial socially; for what is "personal" is shared with "the Other." "Live as citizens," argues the apostle, not just as Roman citizens, but as citizens of the kingdom of God. So he adds, "Conduct yourselves in a manner worthy of the gospel of Christ.... That you stand firm in one spirit, contending as one man for the faith of the gospel" (1:27).

As we have noted, the Stoics idealized human equality but rarely saw it evidenced. For Paul, the "end," or *skopos,* of every Christian is to dwell in the heavenly *politeuma,* as expressive of all those "in Christ," poor or rich, bond or free, male or female, all sharing in "our citizenship ... in heaven" (3:20). For it is not on earthly values we place our hope, but in the life to come. But for present circumstances, Paul had also experienced, "my God will meet all your needs according to his glorious riches in Christ Jesus" (4:19).

STOICISM AND WESTERN CHRISTENDOM

It is, however, a great irony of church history that when New Testament ethics are so at variance with Stoic virtues, nevertheless the virtuous life became—and still is—entrenched in Western, or Latin, Christianity. One reason is the long association of Western theology with classical philosophy. The succession of the governance of the church after the fall of the Roman Empire is another cause, when canon law replaced Roman law and yet was also based upon it.[31] The rediscovery of Latin classical texts in the twelfth century and then the recovery of Aristotle in the next century reinforced their impregnation in Christian thought.

Political uniformity was aided by Stoic uniformity of morals, whereas in the earlier Middle Ages tribal groups, such as the Germans, Anglo-Saxons, Welsh, Irish, Norse, and others, had lived with their differing ethnic styles of "heroic society." So now the "cardinal virtues"—reprioritized as prudence, temperance, justice, and fortitude—helped to moralize medieval society with more homogeneity and to aid in the struggles between secular and ecclesial authorities.[32] The inclusion of apocryphal books within the Bible added their own classical flavor. *The Book of Wisdom*, for example, asserts:

> If one loves justice, the fruits of her works are
> virtues; for she teaches moderation and prudence,
> justice and fortitude, and nothing in life is more
> useful than these.[33]

Assent to this admixture was made uncritically by some of the early Fathers like Ambrose, Tertullian, and Clement of Alexandria, so that a strong Stoic tradition was already in place before the Middle Ages. It thus became a common-sense morality that helped to standardize the natural, moral needs of a society still half pagan.

Medieval "Virtues"

The rediscovery of Cicero and other Latin authors led to a revival in virtue morality. In the twelfth century Alan of Lille, among others, then assumed heretically that the Christian tenets of faith, hope, and charity were also "virtues," to make a moral collation of "seven virtues": the four Stoic cardinal virtues plus the three "theological virtues." This Stoic admixture is what William of Conches taught as mentor to the young prince later to be Henry II: "Conform life to the norm of reason, so that virtue becomes a steady disposition of mind."[34]

Temperance, the prince was taught, should rank as the key virtue. This was the pupil who later inspired the murder of his archbishop, Thomas à Becket! Close to the high altar in Canterbury cathedral where Becket was killed, one can still see engraved in the floor this list of the "sevenfold virtues." Peter Lombard (1100–1160) teaches them in his influential *Sentences,* while Thomas Aquinas (1224–1274) systematized the moral life par excellence under the organization of virtues.[35] (One obvious weakness of this moral system has been in its subjectivity in the ways first Aristotle, then the Stoics, and now the Thomists all selected their point of entry into the moral realm. Each has his own preferences for what is the "key virtue.")

Under the Stoics, as we have seen, prudence or reason comes first, because it informs intelligently all the other virtues. Through it, says Aquinas, "reason is perfected in the cognition of truth." Next comes justice or righteousness, says Aquinas, "a habit whereby a man renders to each his due with constant and perpetual will." Many secondary virtues are then interpreted to follow justice: truthfulness, benevolence, reverence, obedience, forgiveness, gratitude, confession, and so on. Fortitude or courage presupposes human mortality so "the praise of fortitude is dependent upon justice," commented Aquinas, for we may not be so commanded until we are dead! Finally, temperance, or self-control, points to self-forgetfulness and to rational self-restraint.[36]

Emphasis on the Rational

Ever since, Thomist moralists have extolled the rationale and legality of the virtuous life as reflective of human choice and will, as well as of goal-setting, of the benefit of acquired habits of establishing norms of behavior, of seeing the possibilities of growth and change, and of being effective to combat vice.[37] What is fundamental to this metaethical system of the virtuous life is the prevailing influence of Augustine's interpretation of human beings made in the image of God (the *imago Dei*) as reflected in their rational nature. Boethius (ca. 480–524) confirmed the interpretation by defining the human being as "an individual substance of a rational nature."[38]

In particular, this tendency of thought eclipsed the personal presence of the Holy Spirit and of the three persons of the Trinity. Thus a rationalistic ethic of virtue, penance, moral contract, and the emphasis upon the human rather than the divine agency through the stages of purgation, illumination, and union paralyzed the church until the Reformation.

STOICISM AND THE REFORMERS

In the interplay of the renewal of classicism and Augustinianism during the Renaissance and the Reformation,[39] Stoicism became more influential than ever. Instead of literary fragments of Stoic writings, now whole texts were reproduced. Erasmus (1466–1536) edited a careful edition of all of Seneca's works (1515–1529). Seneca's writings, he observed, "are wonderfully stimulating and excite one to enthusiasm for a life of moral integrity."[40] As a young man, John Calvin (1509–1564) wrote a commentary on one of Seneca's texts (1532) "to vindicate his cause and restore him to his proper place of dignity."[41] Huldrych Zwingli (1484–1531) called Seneca a spiritual leader for all times and quoted him extensively in his own works.[42] Martin Bucer (1519–1605) also drew heavily from Seneca's works. Puritan scholars at Oxford and Cambridge, including John Owen (1616–1683), imbibed him deeply while fully aware he was a pagan.

However, T. S. Eliot, as we see in the quotation at the beginning of this chapter, noted that the Stoic appeal is particularly strong in periods of rapid change and ensuing confusion. Stoicism's motive is always for an ethic of rational control, the search for order in societal chaos, the central role of moral admonition in education, and the application of moral egalitarianism in a hierarchical society. This is a spirit that resists religious tyranny effectively. But the great shortcoming of the Reformation, as of much evangelicalism today, was its naive expectation that the majority of people would be transformed morally by doctrinal enlightenment, frequently in an unquestioned Stoic spirit.[43]

Luther's Polemic against Stoicism

In contrast, Martin Luther (1483–1546), who as an Augustinian monk had inherited the dead weight of the virtuous life, was much more outspoken against Stoicism, whether it came from popular religiosity or from sophisticated Erasmian scholarship. Indeed, his language is extreme, calling Stoics "those sevenfold asses," an illusion to the false collation of the four cardinal and three theological virtues. Such a moral confusion, he observed, is "a kind of wise man who has never existed in the universe." Frequently, in his works, he couples "Stoics and monks" together. He reacts all the more strongly against the Stoic's *apatheia,* for he says, "They completely divest a man of wrath and emotions ... so they seem to be strangers to every human emotion and human feeling."[44] However, Luther could also be indiscriminating between the influences of neo-Platonism and of Stoicism in the ascetic life of the monks.[45]

But not everyone heard Luther. The Elizabethan playwrights—Chapman, Kyd, and Marston—were all Senecan. But Shakespeare makes Stoicism much more integral with his depiction of the human nature of his characters. Individualism and the vice of pride or jealousy are, of course, replete with dramatic possibility for the great dramatists. Compound this dramatic life with the Montaigne spirit of skepticism, the Machiavellian attitude of cynicism, the lingering Augustinian inwardness, and a new appreciation of meditation, and we can understand the further popularization of Stoicism in the seventeenth century.[46]

George Herbert's Courtly Polemic

It is against this courtly Stoicism that George Herbert (1593–1633) is a Christian mentor comparable with the spirit of Fénelon more than a generation later. Indeed, he has been called "God's courtier," for he knew all the tricks of self-serving survival amid royal tyranny.[47] As a friend of Charles I and public orator of Cambridge University, his job was to please patrons with eloquence and courtesy, within a socially well-connected family. Yet he turned his back upon his social opportunities and worldly ambitions to catechize a rural church community in Christian courtesy. He does this with wit, teasingly, paradoxically, to humble, correct, and challenge us, so that we can learn the conflicting mysteries of "sin and love," of what is humanly self-contained, and of what is divinely outgoing in relationships to others.[48] So he leaves us embedded in a metaphysical world that we can see only by gospel faith, as interpreted through the eye, rather than merely seeing idolatrously and rationalistically with the eye.[49]

In naked simplicity he dedicates his art as not his own achievement but God's grace to him:

> Lord, my first fruits present themselves to Thee;
> Yet not mine neither: for from Thee they came,
> And must return. Accept them and me ...[50]

In the ornate style of seventeenth-century poetry, Herbert presents entrance through "the Church Porch" as by the cleansing of one's Stoic spirit. These ethical injunctions are preparatory for entering God's presence.

Beware of lust: it doth pollute and foul whom God
in Baptism washed with his own blood.
Take not his name, who made thy mouth, in vain.
Do all things like a man, not sneakingly: think the
king sees thee still; for his King does.
Envy not greatness: for thou mak'st thereby thyself
the worse, and so the distance greater.
All worldly joys go less to the one joy of doing
kindnesses.
Sum up at night, what thou hast done by day; and
in the morning, what though hast to do Dress
and undress thy soul: mark the decay and
growth of it [that is, keep a twice-daily check on
one's devotions before God].

By the altar of sacrifice, then, one proceeds into the
Christian faith, where in brokenness one learns how
hard one's heart is in the presence of God. Whatever the
philosophers may have explored of the external world,
"measur'd mountains, fathom'd the depth of seas, of
states and kings, ... yet there are two vast spacious
things, / which to measure it doth more behove: / yet
few there are that sound them: Sin and Love." Herbert
is right: None of the Stoics I have quoted have examined in any way sin and love, for only in the Easter
event and in "the church's mystical repast" of the
Eucharist can we find their meaning.

But as every Christian will find, the new life in
Christ may first "entice to Thee my heart," and "out of
my stock of natural delights" it is "augmented with Thy
gracious benefits." That is to say, Christian grace is
mixed with Stoic autonomy. Next comes "affliction," to
refine the dross within us. Then, "Lord, I confess my sin
is great; / great is my sin." "Yet take Thy way; for thy
way is best: / stretch or contract me Thy poor debtor."

Affliction continues to reoccur in the poet's life (as it does in ours): "My thoughts are all a case of knives, / wounding my heart / with scatter'd smart." "Oh help, my God! Let not their plot / kill them and me, / and also Thee / who art my life." Moreover, the contrariness of the human heart remains: "For I do praise Thee, yet I praise Thee not: / my prayers mean Thee, yet my prayers stray: / I would do well, yet sin the band hath got: / my soul doth love Thee, yet it loves delay. / I cannot skill of these my ways."

This is a more realistic description of what goes on in our lives than the portraiture of the cardinal virtues can ever convey. When conscience pricks or one is "struggling with a peevish heart," "the bloody cross of my dear Lord / is my physic and my sword." Indeed, "Jesu is in my heart, his sacred name / is deeply carved there." Love is the climax of the Christian's life, as his or her passion is the feast of love, where "you must sit down, says Love, and taste my meat: / so I did sit and eat."

Stoicism is one's perception of oneself by oneself and of how one can control one's own passions. But Herbert's preoccupation is with how we can grow in God's perception of us, to correct our basic self-misunderstanding when we are only occupied with ourselves. Further, the Christian life is not the Christian's choice, but a response to God's choosing us, even though the vicissitudes of Christian living may go on reflecting the bad choices we continue to make.

Christ is "my joy, my life, my crown," says Herbert, who becomes indifferent even to his own art: "The fineness which a hymn or psalm affords, / is, when the soul unto the lines accords. Whereas if th' heart be moved, / although the verse by somewhat scant, / God doth supply the want." He concludes his anti-Stoical polemic:

We must confess, that nothing is our own.
Then I confess that He my succor is:
But to have nought is ours, not to confess
That we have nought. I stood amaz'd at this,
Much troubled, till I heard a friend express,
That all things were more ours by being His.

(From *The Holdfast*)

Jonathan Edwards and American Stoic Religiosity

While George Herbert's posture is powerful in its simplicity against classical Stoicism, shortly after him René Descartes (1596–1650) gave Stoicism a radical new thrust. Instead of being empowered by an external vision of natural order, the Cartesian system located the moral realm within human beings as a development upon *oikeiosis*. Descartes assumed we have a remarkable degree of voluntary control over our passions. As mentor of Queen Regina of Sweden, he affirmed:

> Free will is in itself the noblest thing we can have because it makes us in a certain manner equal to God and exempts us from being his subjects; and so its rightful use is the greatest of all the goods we possesss.[51]

Indeed, he grew in confidence that "we can know and will effectively. For we always have the power to avoid, or indirectly to avoid, or to remove a passion by an appropriate act of will."[52] Reason has now become an instrument to control the desires. In this way Descartes created a new rational inwardness that induces instrumental consciousness, just as we hear now the frequent boast, "I can fix that!" But when the whole of reality becomes more and more mechanized by "techniques," the soul dies, argues William Barrett.[53]

John Locke (1632–1704) further intensified the reification or abstraction of the mind, even more than Descartes. Locke rejected all goal-oriented consciousness, upon which the classical philosophers had based their understanding. He assumed knowledge is both from the senses and from intuitive intelligence. From this he argued knowledge is not genuine unless you develop it yourself. This led to a prominent teaching of the Enlightenment: the autonomy of the self and its revolt against all traditions and authorities. Thus, while the Stoics had always urged, "Follow nature," and Descartes had corrected this to "Follow your own moral reason," now Locke advocated this rational pursuit of knowledge that was being defined as being "scientific."

Edwards' Polemics against Stoicism

Nowhere was the thought of Descartes and Locke more embraced than in North America. Opportunely, Jonathan Edwards (1703–1758), as one of the greatest intellectual of the century that followed, faced and challenged this mindset. But the neo-Stoic legacy of Descartes and Locke remains strong in American culture, with its passion to organize and to pursue the right to happiness in moral autonomy. Edwards critiqued the virtuous life more brilliantly and conclusively than perhaps any other Christian thinker before him. This he did, not so much as a conscious polemic against pagan Stoicism directly, but in its by-product within Christendom of a broadly diffused semi-Pelagianism of self-effort in individual morality, or even the vaguely termed antinomian spirit of "works-righteousness."

In an age of the growing adulation of science, Edwards sought to interpret creation in its beauty before God. Holiness is, in fact, the highest beauty, so that the "sense" of the beauty of God is the highest good mankind can experience, he argued. While others were beginning to see only a mechanistic universe, he saw the harmony and beauty of God's love as manifest in all reality. Where deists abstracted such categories as "nature" and "substance," he saw the personalness of the triune God of grace, the God who is communal and desires communion with man.

Like Pascal, Edwards recognized that what is counterfeit in religiosity is that it has no "spiritual knowledge," no "sense of the heart"—that is, no personal sense of God's intimate, abiding, and loving presence within oneself. This sense is only experienced as the ineffable beauty of God, which engenders "gracious affections" consistent with God's Word. This is the Holy Spirit's special work in the Christian to convert and transform our autonomous consciousness, so we will love and appreciate Him as beyond all other. This is directly a sanctification of the will, to communicate new affections and desires, something Descartes never dreamed of, for self-consciousness now becomes consciousness of the Other. This is also a sanctifying of the reasoning faculty to remove prejudices and to give new light beyond oneself and so to see and interpret aright.

Thus the "affections" for Edwards, far from being irrational, are the very point where the objective, divine reality binds and controls human consciousness.[54] Release, then, from the inward curvature of the Cartesian sinful self enables the believer to keep free from errors, not merely by logical clarity but primarily by holiness of heart. For what is essential is the gift of God's Spirit, by which to perceive the attractiveness of God's goodness and beauty and thus of the loveliness of true virtue.

Thus in his work *The Nature of True Virtue*, written in 1754 and published posthumously, Edwards refers to moral excellence, or *aretê*, no longer like the Heroic or Stoic interpretations but as expressive of God alone.[55] While deists like

Hutcheson and Shaftesbury were busily arguing for a morality that could be explained without reference to religion—as many do today—Edwards sought to demonstrate that the love of God is the necessary context for all truly moral acts. He gives two criteria for what is *true virtue.*

True Virtue

First, he argues that all true virtue depends upon divine benevolence. For it is this which gives a person a new sensibility, a new disposition, a new sense of seeing God in all things, which engenders a new affection for God rather than oneself. Religious conversion, then, is a prerequisite for a real knowledge of the realities of faith. This is a personal, sensible, cognitive, experiential knowledge, much more than what is merely notional.

Second, virtue is subordinate to Being, that is, to God Himself. It is a "general" and not a "particular" beauty, for it is expressive of God's Being as the ultimate of all beings. This is where Edwards would flatly contradict the morality of Stoicism, which selects a secondary category of values, such as fortitude in one culture, or prudence in another, or justice in a third, by which to construct the "moral life." No, asserts Edwards, all moral principles are subordinate to God Himself, not to a culture as the archetype of all relational existence and personal reality. Echoing Anselm's question, he asked: *Cur deus homo?* "Why did God become man?" Because, said Edwards, God's own happiness consists "in communion."[56] It is the triune nature of God Himself, as Father, Son, and Holy Spirit, surrounded by angels, saints in heaven, and saints in their becoming on earth, who express and promise personalness, and irrevocably deny any notion of self-contained individuals.

Edwards' Example in David Brainerd

The essentially personal interpretation of Edwards' godly

virtue is demonstrated further in his *Life of David Brainerd* (1749), written five years before *True Virtue*. In the preface he writes: "There are two ways of recommending true religion and virtue to the world: the one by doctrine and precept, and the other by history and example. Both are abundantly used in the holy Scriptures."[57] In David Brainerd (1718–1747), a missionary to the Indians whom Edwards was to follow into the wilderness late in Brainerd's life, Edwards recognized these characteristics, both as a penetrating scholar and as a saintly character. All that Edwards had written in his treatises on the nature of true religion, on the signs of gracious affections, as well as on true virtue, he actually saw lived out in his young friend, who died as consistently as he had lived in Edwards' own home. So Edwards echoes and repeats many of the key themes of his works biographically, as he saw them personally lived out in this saintly young man.

To a high degree, Brainerd expressed "evangelical humiliation, consisting of his own utter insufficiency, with an answerable disposition and frame of heart." Brainerd had a meek and quiet spirit, a tender conscience, a joyful heart, and was a social person. In his sermon at Brainerd's funeral Edwards said, "His religion did not consist of experience without practice, and the liveliness of his doctrine of grace, as applied to the heart, were clearly apparent in him."[58]

Brainerd's *Journals* and Edwards' teachings had a remarkable impact on the Christian public. They were read by William Carey (1761–1834), who as a result was inspired to give his life as a missionary to India. Henry Martyn (1781–1812) read them and went to India. Robert Murray M'Cheyne (1813–1843) was influenced by Martyn to write *Notes on Henry Martyn's Life* (1838), as well as to reflect deeply on Brainerd's life. All three—Brainerd, Martyn, and Murray M'Cheyne—lived only twenty-nine years, yet their moral influence was outstanding.[59] In turn, Andrew Bonar wrote the *Memoirs of M'Cheyne* (1844), which on the centenary of M'Cheyne's birth was reissued by Alexander Whyte as one of the great classics of devotion. The continuity of this genre of a life given to God, enveloped in prayer, and expressive of God's grace is perhaps unique in the literature of the last two centuries, replete as they have been with innumerable biographies. What M'Cheyne wrote in his memoirs for 1833 could be said to all these Christian mentors:

> My heart is fixed—my heart is fixed:
> No other love shall come betwixt
> My soul and God alone.[60]

THE BIBLE CALLS IT SIN

As we saw at the beginning of this chapter, Stoicism is close to Christianity in its development of the idea of a conscience, in developing personal disciplines, and in being rational about the moral life of humankind. Yet for this very reason it is so dangerous as the agent of institutionalized Christendom. For what was "Pelagian" for Augustine in the fourth century or was "Arminian" for Edwards in the eighteenth century is still expressive of the secular technocratic spirit of our religious free enterprise today. At their core is the same self-reliant, self-sufficient spirit—what the Stoics called *oikeiosis* and what Western society identifies as "self-sufficiency." The Bible calls it sin, the autonomy of the self that is blind to the need of divine grace.

The contemporary climate is therapeutic, not religious.
People today hunger not for personal salvation, let alone for the
restoration of an earlier golden age, but for the feeling, the momentary
illusion, of personal well-being, health, and psychic security.
—Christopher Lasch[1]

THE SECULAR
PSYCHOTHERAPEUTIC
MENTOR

If the Heroic mentor may be applied to civic leadership in a small city-state, and the Stoic mentor is for the moral leadership of the rulers of empires, then the Therapeutic mentor is democratically for a whole society. Indeed, contemporary therapeutic society has revived the role of a mentor on a scale never before witnessed in human history.

Imagine a world in which the basic tenets of science are suddenly lost to humankind. Such a situation, argues Alasdair MacIntyre, is parallel to a moral world left stranded after virtue has lost all relevance. That is to say, both are unimaginable to those who are still either scientists or classical humanists. Now imagine a world in which modern counseling or psychotherapy does not exist. It is nearly impossible. For therapy has become largely a Western substitute for religion.

How people think and communicate about themselves and others; how they cope with the myriad and variety of problems they face; indeed how they identify, esteem, and compare themselves, are all contingent upon the metaethical systems they're living under. The metaethical systems are integrated within their cultural settings. We cannot imagine the Roman Empire without Stoicism. We cannot think of late modernity without psychotherapy. Yet is secular therapeutic culture only a revised edition of Stoicism? This is what we will now explore.

With Sigmund Freud's introduction of psychoanalysis at the end of the nineteenth century, there came a new assumption. Whereas all previous civilizations had been grounded upon religious foundations, Christian or otherwise, now society would become wholly secular. That therapy could replace religion was a claim the classical world could never conceive possible. Thus when Freud (1856–1939) first introduced the term *psychoanalysis* in 1896, another idea was born as revolutionary as the earlier fall of the Bastille with the enthronement of reason in 1789, or of the later fall of the Berlin Wall in 1989, heralding the demise of communism as a rational ideology.

After 1896, psychotherapy flourished to promote the substitution of Rational Man, created by the Enlightenment, with Psychological Man—self-contained and secular. This new worldview transmutes "the moral" to "the therapeutic"; "sin" into "mental sickness";[2] and "God" into "self-projection." It raises the role of the mentor into a new visual prominence, never before so authoritative. It is as if the new goals of self-realization, self-expression, self-fulfillment, and the discovery of authenticity in self-understanding require ironically the social support of "the Other" as never before. The secular prayer is now: "Help me become more egocentric. Amen!"

Yet Religion Persists

Religion, however, cannot be so readily dismissed, even though traditional expressions of it may be denied and repressed. Even the attempt to deny validity to the religious experiences of others is a "religious" attempt. "The field of religion," observes John MacMurray, "is the field of personal experience," for "at the heart of religion lies an activity of communion or fellowship." It implied "self-transcendence which must mean the capacity to have one's interest in another person."[3] Indeed, psychologists are impressed by the analogy of the behavior of small children under parental nurture and authority and adults' attitudes to God and prayer. For a child may not easily distinguish authoritative figures, whether God or a parent. This emotional confusion may remain subconsciously in an adult's attitude toward God. Thus, setting aside its distinctive dogmas, this is what religion is: the field of personal behavior in the transcendence of personal relationships.

The pursuit of "reality" is also a religious quest, whether it is merely limited to empirical reality or enlarged to interpret divine categories. The therapeutic category of being a "well-adjusted personality" and "self-fulfilled" is as religious as being "born again." The "guruism" of the early mentors of psychotherapy, the authoritarian dogma of unproven claims, the self-confidence of its practitioners, all helped to fill a void in the instrumental world of techniques, its intense empiricism, and the materialism of modern life. It has justifiably been called "the triumph of the therapeutic," to which Lasch alludes in this chapter's introductory quotation.

AMERICANS, THE MOST
PSYCHOLOGICAL OF PEOPLES

It is no accident that the United States, in particular, became so obsessively therapeutic. As we have seen, it embraced René Descartes and John Locke as its early mentors. Descartes promoted the radical shift from the external world to the internal, intrapsychic realm of the mind. A scientific view of oneself was further objectified by Locke in the introspective observation of one's psychic happenings he called "reflection,"[4] leading later to the disciplines of psychology and psychotherapy. A radical view of the self could then lead to its remaking, allowing one to take charge of one's own representations.

Written into the Declaration of Independence was the right to "the pursuit of happiness" as a mandate of citizenship. For new settlers in the "Land of the Free," this individualistic ethic was very appealing. Already, early in the nineteenth century, Alexis de Tocqueville (1805–1859) could see America had become a unique social laboratory for "the rise of the individual." All these trends were contributing to the promise of becoming "scientist-to-oneself," a "self-therapist" indeed. As Robert Jenson put it: "Then I seek the psychic and social explanations of my behavior, as if some other will than mine were therein displayed, and summon the appropriate technician to undertake the repair."[5]

THE INFLUENCE OF PSYCHOANALYSIS

Even so, when Freud visited the United States in 1909, he was surprised at the popular enthusiasm and ready acceptance with which his antireligious message was received. Was this not the most Puritan of nations? he asked himself. What he had not appreciated was that the "genteel" and "religious" traditions of Puritan and Victorian ideals were breaking down fast. New forces of social change were at work: journalistic muckrakers, literary "realists," social protestors, feminists, and bohemians were ready to embrace Freudian ideas. There was little clinical evidence available for what he was preaching, so professional psychologists and psychiatrists could have been critical of his ideas. In fact, Freudian ideas were becoming so integral to the spirit of the age that the zeitgeist became an indirect channel for Freud's rapid influence on professional psychology. As one study on this influence in America states: "Freud's influence was being inescapably forced upon psychology by various public and professional pressures in a period of great social and moral upheaval in the United States."[6]

Nineteenth-century liberal theology in America had insisted that health and happiness—almost built into the revolutionary optimism of the American character—are the reward for clean living and high thinking. So those who turned to psychoanalysis welcomed it as a mind-cure, another system of self-improvement. Of course, Freud saw through the sham of Victorian sexual scruples, which were afraid to face openly the sexual passions and their perversions. He interpreted psychopathology as a product of bodily urges and social conflicts. These led to self-deceptions that split the individual into repressed and fragmented parts, with the so-called "ego," "superego," and "id" at war. Without the repressive tactics of the superego—a substitute for the Stoic's conscience—self-destruction and indeed destruction of society would ensue. Yet Freud believed the conflict could still be rationally managed through the technique of psychoanalysis. As Paul Ricoeur has observed, psychoanalysis is thus a "hermeneutic of suspicion," seeking to break through the facade of bourgeois conventions into the snake pit of the dark side of human existence.[7]

As Stoicism interpreted the passions aroused by erotic love as serpents in the soul, so Freud now interpreted the sexual drive as the focus of central concern. The centerpiece of his theories was that of "the unconscious." Like Columbus, Freud claimed proudly that it was "a stretch of new country, which has been reclaimed from popular belief and mysticism."[8] Not that others had not already speculated about it. Epicurus (341–270 BC) understood that the false beliefs that disturb life do not lie on the surface of the self, but deeply unconsciously within oneself.[9] That is why personal narrative has been such a challenge to a shallow Aristotelianism ever since. But Freud significantly enlarged the role of the "dynamic unconsciousness" as a kind of battleground of the three modern forces of the human condition: instincts, rationality, and culture. As Philip Cushman has shrewdly observed, "By uncovering how the *content* of desire is shaped, and how the *object* of desire is constructed, Freud's analysis had the potential to become a deconstructive practice," to discredit the cultural fiction of self-contained individualism.[10]

In this way, Freud sought to reduce neurotic misery, even if it was to return merely to everyday common unhappiness. This was a less noble vision than the Greek therapists sought in having a "happy spirit" (*eudaimonia*). But most fatefully, Freud's rationalistic bias led him to leave alone the unconscious as a realm for cognitive pursuits, rather than as an embodied reality. Thus he steered the whole psychoanalytic enterprise away from biomedical approaches into a void of mythic speculations. This fateful decision eventually would spell its demise within the increasingly scientific medical field.

American Freudian Mentorship

In the late twenties and throughout the thirties, American intellectuals coupled Freud with Karl Marx as two radicals to their liking. Then came the concord of Hitler and Stalin, which drove disillusioned Marxists into the Freudian camp. European refugees also poured into America, claiming as "Europeans" to have more Freudian orthodoxy as practitioners of psychoanalysis. The result was more rigid Freudianism in American academies than occurred in England or France. As a later disenchanted literary scholar, Frederick Crews, confessed: "I came to the painful conclusion that Freudianism ... from the very beginning ... was a way of reaching conclusions that you had already reached"—that is, a self-authenticating approach to knowledge.[11] Yet as Crews observed:

> Freud was seen as a progressive, when in fact he was fatalistic, pessimistic, sardonic, and determinist in his orientation. It was a subject of amusement for Freud ... that the country that welcomed psychoanalysis most warmly was the one that misunderstood it most thoroughly.[12]

The creation of mass culture in America, combined with the transformation of psychoanalysis from a clinical method into a cult of personal health and self-fulfillment, endlessly widened the applicability of therapy. Perhaps Freud feared what might happen, for he called psychoanalysis "the impossible science." It fed into the social trends of the twentieth century, in particular to the popular notion of progress by change; the insatiable appetite for cure-alls and placebos, simple solutions, and grand schemes easily explained; an unshakeable faith in techniques to solve problems; and seeing *telos*, which originally referred to the end encoded by its nature to reach its fulfillment, now reduced to meaning only cause and effect. Psychotherapy fits into modern human biases even more deeply than Stoicism ever could, unless we interpret it as the new American Stoicism. The poet W. H. Auden summed up Freud's influence well when he observed:

> To us he is more than a person
> Now, but a whole climate of opinion,
> Under whom we conduct our differing lives.[13]

Today "therapy" has become the dominant idiom of discussion, along with the weather and the daily news. It is like a renewed climate of Gnosticism that originally challenged early Christianity, elusive yet so persuasive. This is particularly true of modern-day Jungian therapists, the followers of Freud's early associate Carl Jung, who are prone to Gnostic religious leanings[14] to which Freud himself denied any significance. However, after the human potential movement of the 1970s, even Freudian psychoanalysis overreached itself when it became not just a way of "fixing" things, but actually claimed to provide a more fulfilled state of being.

Sources of Freudian Disenchantment

Beginning in the late 1970s, some clinicians began to be disenchanted with the lack of results in psychoanalysis. Jeffrey Masson wrote negatively in *The Assault on Truth: Freud's Suppression of the Seduction Theory* (1984), as well as *A Hundred Years of Therapy and the World Is Getting Worse* (1985).[15] Freud's own destructive relations with his daughter, Anna, were exposed.[16] At the personal level, both Freud and Jung have been indicted as "gurus"—not mentors—with hidden powers over their followers. Gurus are not accountable as true mentors should be, nor do they make such wide-sweeping claims, so the retreat of psychoanalysis into the vagueness of claims to be "a science" has drawn forth the wrath of hard scientists like P. D. Medawar. Freud's use of the unconscious has been critically assessed by Ernest Gellner, among others.[17] Biomedical advances with the use of critical drugs are moving aside the whole clinical claims of psychoanalysis. More resistant is the cultural psychoanalytic mind-set as literary critics seek for "coherence, consistency and configuration"[18] or historians look for "historical truth" in human motivation.

Freud's Intellectual Ancestry

Within this "post-Freudian climate," it is helpful to look back and see, not how innovative and radical Freud appeared as a mentor to his contemporaries, but how indebted he was to the nineteenth-century Enlightenment. Freud's intellectual ancestry is traceable to Ludwig Feuerbach (1804–1872), who began as a theologian but ended as a philosophical atheist. He introduced the idea of religious "projection,"[19] so that God was explained away as the projected desire or need of mankind. Arthur Schopenhauer (1788–1860), also hostile to the Christian faith, denied the primacy of reason and accorded it to the will. He interpreted the will as wild, blind, and uncontrollable striving. This was the ancestry of Freud's id, well illustrated in Joseph Conrad's novel *The Heart of Darkness* (1902). Friedrich Nietzsche (1844–1900), scorning human contentment with "the Good" as a dead end, asserted instead "the will to power." Christianity, grounded on love not willfulness, he interpreted as a "slave morality."

Out of this murky heritage, Freud collected and created his own pessimistic, Gnostic psychoanalysis—Gnostic because of the dualism between mind and body and between good and evil. He started as a neurophysiologist in the study of hysteria, which he linked to the repression of painful reminiscences. Indeed, from his own family he interpreted childhood experiences of sexual conflict and abuse. Sex became the meeting point around which his psychoanalysis was to develop. For as his bias as a medical scientist was toward the pathological and instinctual, sex—being both hormonal and also the seat of powerful emotions—bridged the gap between mind and body. Sex was also responsible for many purely psychological manifestations such as thoughts, fantasies, and dreams. This is why Freud introduced the popular theory that an inadequate sex life is the chief cause of neuroses. It has also been the focus of much abuse in the history of a significant number of client-therapist relationships.[20]

Transference and Projection

Transference was another key element in Freud's method. He first introduced the notion of transference in 1895 after recognizing the negative ways in which patients were aggressive, distrustful, and competitive toward him. He taught them this was a mirror of their own primary relationships in childhood. At first, he interpreted this negative behavior as the unconscious wish to disrupt the therapeutic relationship, but over time he came to appreciate the evidence he believed this provided of the patient's formative relationships. Instead of being dispensed with, these behaviors were now seen to be vitally important. He also began to see that alongside positive transference—that is, of good relationships transferred to the therapist—there might also be negative feelings transferred to the therapist that were equally important to analyze.[21]

Transference became an indispensable concept for the understanding of the analytic process. Feelings of incongruity between client and therapist are often a vital starting point. Transference can also reflect on countertransference, which may occur with the therapist, a danger signal to the therapist to avoid falling into a false situation. Of course, it can be argued that transference and countertransference are generally happening all the time in all human relationships.

Akin to transference was the application of projection, which, following on Feuerbach, Freud developed to use in his "illusion theory of religion." But he abused the use of this principle well beyond the legitimate bounds of an objective discipline. As one of his own earliest mentors, Josef Breuer, noted: "Freud is a man given to absolute and exclusive formulations: this is a psychical need, which in my opinion, leads to excessive generalizations."[22]

Freud developed the theory of the id, following on Schopenhauer, interpreting it as the source of all individual energy. The ego, meanwhile, was weakness, living on borrowed forces.[23] It was characteristic of his predominantly pessimistic view of human nature that the "pleasure principle," on which so much of his thought depended, was actually much more the avoidance of pain than the pursuit of happiness. So the mentors of the classical schools of philosophy were far more optimistic than the brooding Freud. While the id represented what was going on unconsciously and therefore was more instinctual, the ego represented consciousness, operating with secondary processes such as reason, common sense, and the power to delay immediate responses to external stimuli. He asserted that the ego was first and foremost a bodily ego,[24] more expressive of the needs and sensations of the body than of the mind or spirit.

Freud interpreted the neurotic "I" as like a rider on a horse who thinks he knows where he is going. In fact the rider is helplessly at the whims of the horse. It is a poor model for self-esteem, which may explain the addictive tendencies of many clients to prolong their therapy and to live vicariously through their mentors. The superego he referred to the external world that monitors or "polices" by "parental conditioning" and other Pavlovian influences. No wonder we have reaped such a societal distrust of parenthood today!

The Destructive Instinct

In sharpest contrast to the biblical view that God's love is at the source of reality, Freud stated that "hate as a relation to objects is older than love," another Gnostic conclusion. This is analogous to the cosmogonies of the ancient Near East, which believe that in the beginning there was chaos. At first Freud interpreted aggression as a sadistic aspect of the sexual instinct, but later he came to believe that it was an instinct independent of the sexual life. In his study "Instincts and Their Vicissitudes" (1915), in which he expressed these ideas, he applied the concept of "instinct" naively, as comparable to that of animals, as something innate in the human being. In current thought, instinct is dissolved within the "genetic constitution" of or the "environmental influences" on human beings. But for Freud, there were two instinctual poles: the death or aggressive instinct and the life or self-preservation instinct, like two giants warring within us: Death and Eros.

Having thus "explained" the existence of the "destructive instinct," Freud then explored the ways the superego—which he equated with civilization—imposed control over the ego. He made much of the irrational severity with which the superego operated, perhaps as a projection of his own parental background. It is in this context that he introduced his understanding of narcissism and of the neurosis of attachment. He listed a variety of ways in which objects are chosen, to focus upon Narcissus and Echo or Attachment ever since then.[25] As is now well-known, Narcissus was the youth with such a sense of self-depletion that he fell in love with the image of himself reflected in a pool of water. Echo, his female companion, was his alter ego and also self-depleted, but responding as an echo of Narcissus's own voice in neurotic attachment. Such forms of self-absorption are expressive of a low sense of the self, although we may superficially condemn both their self-centeredness and their neurotic attachment.

The Value of Dreams

Freud claimed that the importance and interpretation of dreams was "the most valuable of all the discoveries he had made."[26] But in interpreting them only as the disguised, hallucinatory fulfillment of the suppressed wishes of neurotic people, contemporary dream theories in terms of information processes have far enlarged the theory of the function of dreaming.[27] Dreams are now recognized to be more diffused and to play a multitude of tasks and responses for normal people.[28]

CARL JUNG: THE GNOSTIC MENTOR

While Freud assumed a Gnostic attitude concerning the

permanence of evil in the world, his mentee, Carl Gustav Jung (1875–1961), has been much more dangerous to Christians. He overtly espoused Platonism, Gnosticism, and the occult—neo-pagan teachings that helped breed what is now called New Age religion. As Philip Rieff has observed: "Theologians might well consider ... who is more dangerous: Freud or Jung? Better a forthright enemy than an untrustworthy friend."[29]

While Freud's modest objective was to diminish neurotic unhappiness, Jung claimed for this therapy a "Universal Cure" and indeed a recovery of the primal and universal within the category of religion.[30] Early in Jung's life, he began to develop a messianic streak. Distanced by his parents' troubled marriage, he never could respect his father, a Lutheran pastor, whose weak, liberal faith was ineffective and who was hospitalized as a psychiatric patient from time to time.[31] Was this why Jung became a psychiatrist? His mother was strong, warm, close to her son, although with contradictory elements in her personality. Does this explain why Jung was fascinated by paradox and polarities? As a lonely boy he fantasized he had a figure Philemon in his inner life, who came to him in dreams as a mentor with superior insight, certainly more than his father's religion. He fantasized that God gave him direct revelations. He began to attend séances with his female cousin and later with his mother and other women. From there he indulged in astrology, Eastern religions, and the Völkisch writings of Richard Wagner (1814–1883), who later inspired the Nazis.[32]

Freud and Jung

After knowing of each other's work for some years, Freud and Jung met in 1907, and their association became quickly extraordinary indeed. Freud became more than a father figure for Jung; he was "Moses" to

Jung's "Joshua." According to Fritz Wittel, a friend of Jung during this period, "Freud's face beamed whenever he spoke of Jung, saying: 'This is my beloved son in whom I am well pleased.'"[33] It was as if in blasphemous fantasy Freud thought of himself as God and of Jung as Jesus Christ.

Before their break in 1912 and 1913, Jung remembered what Freud had urged him to believe:

> I can still recall vividly how Freud said to me, "My dear Jung, promise me never to abandon the sexual theory. This is the most essential thing of all. You see we must make a dogma out of it, an unshakeable bulwark." He said that to me with great emotion in the tone of a father saying, "And promise me this one thing, my dear son, that you will go to church every Sunday." In some astonishment, I replied, "A bulwark—against what?" To which he replied, "Against the black tide of mud"—and here he hesitated for a moment, then added—"of occultism."[34]

Freud's sexual theory seemed critical at the time for his "materialistic science," but he saw that the "darkness" first explored by Schopenhauer was now being further released by Jung's neo-paganism. He was, indeed, looking into a hellish abyss. So Freud was warning Jung, but Jung could not see beyond his paternalism.

Jung's Analytical Psychology

Banned from Freud's psychoanalytic circle, Jung then proceeded to develop his own "analytical psychology." He differentiated the attitudes of those "extroverts" who tend to look outward from those of the "introverts" who tend to look inward. He also distinguished four functions of the mind in thinking, feeling, sensation, and intuition, to establish the basis for his types of personality in 1921. This schema has been popularized since then, especially by the well-known Myers-Briggs personality tests. But his esoteric religious views have largely been ignored by secular therapists, other than those who are attempting to reinvent religious traditions for themselves, as he did, and as New Agers and their therapists are doing now.

OTHER THERAPEUTIC MODELS

In the latter half of the twentieth century, three other major categories of therapy arose.

Cognitive-Behavioral Models

The first comprises the cognitive-behavioral models of therapy. These models minimize the role of the unconscious and instead look for patterns of action that may be exposed as debilitating or irrational. They assume there are fundamental relationships between individuals and their environments. Individuals are seen to shape, or be shaped by, the environment. The therapist's intervention is essentially educational and "scientific," to teach specific learning skills and apply them more generally.

One such model, rational emotive behavior therapy (REBT), assumes that human beings have a biological tendency to think "crookedly" or irrationally and so need to be reeducated.[35] Such rationalistic models, as Cartesian quests for pragmatic results, appeal to our technological society. Yet their stress upon the superior knowledge of the therapist, as well as on the replacement of reciprocal relationships with a cognitive self-learning education, tend to overlook many aspects of the human condition. As the normative judge, such a therapist is indeed playing God. Moreover, these models do not critique the irrationality within society so much as in the client, and thus tend to preserve uncritically the cultural blind spots both within the client and the therapist. Critical are the assumptions made about "objectivity," which may cover over beliefs just as spurious as those given by Freud to the unconscious.[36]

Object Relations School

The second category of models is the object relations school, which is a counter to the previous school in that it is far more humanistic. These models are basically derivative of the old psychoanalytic ones, putting their emphasis on emotional mediators. For Freud, the reduction of social stimulation was the chief psychic goal. But he never played with normal children, as Anna, his daughter, did later. Children love to be hugged, tickled, teased, played with—all forms of social stimulation. In England, the object relations school focused attention upon the child in the context of its mother. Donald Winnicott put it this way: "There is no such thing as a baby, for a baby cannot exist without its mother; one can only speak of a mother-baby entity."[37]

With this relational approach, a radical turn took place within psychoanalysis, as a host of issues associated with relational separation began to be explored by psychiatrists such as John Bowlby[38] and Margaret Mahler[39] in the complex parental interactions that affect the development of personhood.

Self-Psychology Movement

Meanwhile, in America, the self-psychology movement emerged, headed by Heinz Kohut. He reinforced the object relations belief by exploring further the interpersonal origin of the "self" and of its growth throughout life. He identified narcissism—with its enormous demand for admiration and attention—and its disorders as the result of inadequate empathy at a pivotal time of life.[40] Kohut emphasized the vital need of an "involved other" in one's life.

Other humanistic schools, however, seemed only to intensify narcissism. The human potential movement in North America and Britain is an obvious example. Instead of studying the unconscious or behavior per se, it emphasized the wholeness of the individual, the freedom of choice, autonomy, uniqueness, and ultimate indefinability. It took up the fundamental view of Abraham Maslow that all human beings have an innate tendency to self-actualize, that is, from the self-awareness of basic needs, consciously striving to fulfill them.

This led to further models such as person-centered therapy, Gestalt therapy, and transactional analysis. Such humanistic models focused experientially upon the "now" of experience, not on the "history of childhood" approach of the older Freudianism. Focus on the "totality" of the client led them away from problem-solving to issues and concerns in the client's experience of life as a whole. This placed responsibility on the client to interpret what is going on. It emphasized the client's freedom to choose how to "be," and by what meanings of life to live by. Such an approach promotes more egalitarian relationships between client and therapist, for it assumes that the curative benefits lie in the therapeutic process itself.[41]

In all therapeutic models, many questionable assumptions are made. How much "change" can we anticipate realistically within ourselves? Why is the therapist's role so important (usually carrying greater expectations than those for other mentors or wise friendships)? Does not the humanistic emphasis on the individual self intensify narcissistic tendencies in all therapy, often in its disregard of other people in our lives? An extreme form of this is illustrated in the Gestalt prayer:

> I do my thing and you do your thing.
> I am not in the world to live up to your expectations.
> And you are not in this world to live up to mine.[42]

It might be unfair to project such extreme solipsistic absurdity on all humanistic therapies, yet the social suspicion remains, in the minds of serious students of contemporary culture, that the existence of a "real self," alone and isolated, out there somewhere, somehow, is only promoting and intensifying broad-scale narcissism in our postmodern world.

THERAPHY AS CULTURAL RECONSTRUCTION

Hence there have been developed a number of other transpersonal approaches to therapy in response to this growing social criticism. How suggestible are patients-clients within therapy? Cause-and-effect theories are powerful in their suggestibility and tend to deepen expectations that are very difficult to correct. Why should therapists be so confident of their own diagnoses, so that patients tend to be molded by the therapist's suggestions and the therapist is also influenced by the patient's eventual belief? As the psychiatrist Karl Jaspers put it, "Therapeutic schools unwittingly foster the phenomena which they cure."[43] The fast rise of multiple personality disorders and the focus on child sexual abuse are interconnected examples of the ways in which media attention generates new fashions in pathological attention.

It is also observable that schools of psychotherapy often mirror social trends, because the therapeutic process is deeply influenced by cultural notions of behavior. After World War I, large corporations used psychology to create the advertising business as a means of "making customers." For example, smoking was advertised as a leisure-time activity for the growing middle class, as "relaxing," "promoting health," and for women it promised "new freedom of expression." Later, industrial psychology was developed to provide social interaction with public relations, labor management, and marketing.

Infant deprivation and anxiety theories begun by Melanie Klein (1882–1960) developed into popular postwar culture around "the empty self," configured to promote consumerism. Then came self-liberation through further consumerism. As Cushman has observed:

> Without the empty self and its characteristic
> interior emptiness and yearning, the economic
> and cultural shape of the postwar era, including
> its youthful bravado, escalating inflation, and
> unquenchable consumer desire, would have
> been unthinkable.[44]

However, the ease with which we can look back and diagnose past fallacies and follies tends to give us a mistaken sense of superiority that has its own blindness. Rather, we should humbly recognize the almost limitless capacity we have for self-deception. Every generation assumes it can probe and discover everything about ourselves, only to discover later how time-bound and enmeshed in our cultures we remained.

Freudianism was resisted in France for a variety of reasons. It was too German in its authoritarianism; it was too anti-Cartesian for Gallic assurance; and for a Latin social way of life, the "sole hero" mentality of Freud did not go down well. Thus it was through an indigenous Freudian heretic, Jacques Lacan (1901–1981), by way of linguistics, that an acceptable psychoanalytic form of consciousness began to flood into France in the 1970s.[45] In the process, other intellectuals highlighted their awareness of Freud's own antisocial bias, responding with a new school of psychology called "inter-individual."

Inter-Individualism

Inter-individualism has given a new emphasis to the diffuse role of human desire. Desire is now interpreted to b what gives rise to the self. Yet, argues René Girard, a human being is a creature who does not know what to desire. It is the vagueness of human desire that results in mimicry as an imitative tendency—as a child will begin to desire what it sees another child desires. Perhaps the child is surrounded with toys, then a rival selects one, which immediately becomes the focus of a contest. Is this what is happening in therapy? "We desire what others desire because we imitate their desires," says Girard.[46]

Thus, far from being autonomous from others, as therapeutic theories in individualistic American theories have promoted, we in fact are acutely dependent on them. Instead of Descartes's dictum, "I think therefore I am," perhaps another phrase applies: "I represent myself to myself, therefore I am."

Yet there is no assurance that such representation is not

illusionary. Thus French intellectuals have revolved full circle, away from Cartesian easy certainty about the self to the contemporary post-Freudian uncertainty. Freud's probings of the complexity of human motivations in the past century provide a springboard for ongoing, profound reflections upon the human identity and its condition.

We cannot assume we know enough about ourselves. We can no longer accept the "grand rational narratives" of the Enlightenment, while Psychological Man is also disenchanted with merely rationalistic communication in place of true friendship. Perhaps, as Michel Henry has pointed out, the immense resonance psychoanalysis has with the contemporary world is because of the idea that the unconscious protects each human from his or her most intimate sense of being; indeed "the unconscious" is the name for the mystery of being human. At the same time, it challenges us all to radical self-reflection, while cautioning us not to be taken in by society's self-generating fictions.[47]

There remains an inherent conflict with psychoanalysis itself. While it demands critical reflection from the client on the one hand, at the same time it assumes the uncritical subjection to the "professional skills" of the therapist on the other hand. This inherent conflict is centered on the key role that transference has always had in therapy. Originally, it was supposed to be used only to analyze early problems in childhood and parenting, so that Freud affirmed that the termination of transference was the goal of analysis.

Yet transference to the therapist continues to happen. For consciously, or unwittingly, therapists encourage dependency. As François Roustang has observed: "Freud was possessed by an uncontrollable need to have disciples and to surround himself with completely devoted disciples."[48] Jung did the same, maintaining all through his life dissatisfaction with everyone else's diagnosis. Both became gurus, as we have seen. Likewise, Lacan created a strong personality cult around himself, even more blatantly than Freud did. What this does is further weaken or even dissolve individuation, when human identity in this century alone has already been attacked so violently and distortedly by a bewildering range of over 240 schools of thought! Perhaps, then, the furtherance of theological anthropology, of interpreting humanity within the realm of transcendence, is the vital issue ahead of us, as we shall now explore further.

Quasi-Religious and Pseudoscientific

From the present impasse in psychoanalysis there is the growing awareness that its founders both fostered and frustrated psychological inquiry. The inherent potential for truthfulness in psychoanalysis is offset by its quasi-religious, pseudoscientific character. As a contemporary critique has concluded, "This implies a complete transformation of the field of psychoanalysis."[49] We are not told what this should be. Perhaps the basic, concealed assumption of psychoanalysis is still that with a better pair of spectacles you can read better literature. Perhaps read better, yes, but read what, concerning the human condition? Objectivity, as such, does not and cannot define the human being. Likewise, to volunteer for therapy, however prolonged it is, is no guarantee one is in touch with personal reality.

Søren Kierkegaard exposes the fallacy of this in one of his parables, a fitting conclusion to this critique of the Therapeutic mentor. A mental patient tests his own sanity by the declaration he makes: "Bang, the earth is round. Why can't one prove to be sanely in possession of his faculties if he tells the truth objectively?" Kierkegaard narrates his parable as follows.

A patient in an institution seeks to escape, and actually succeeds in effecting his purpose by leaping out of the window, when the thought strikes him (shall I say sanely or madly enough?): "When you come to town you will be recognized, and you will at once be brought back here again; hence you need to prepare yourself fully to convince everyone by the objective truth of what you say, that all is in order as far as your sanity is concerned." As he walks along and thinks about this, he sees a ball lying on the ground, picks it up, and puts it into the tail pocket of his coat. Every step he takes the ball strikes him, politely speaking, on his hinder parts, and every time it thus strikes him he says: "Bang, the earth is round." He comes to the city, and at once calls on one of his friends; he wants to convince him that he is not crazy, and therefore walks back and forth, saying continually: "Bang, the earth is round." Does the asylum still crave yet another sacrifice for this opinion, as in the time when all men believed it to be flat as a pancake? Or is a man who hopes to prove that he is sane, by uttering a generally accepted and generally respected objective truth, insane? And yet it was clear to the physician that the patient was not yet cured; though it is not to be thought that the cure would consist of getting him to accept the opinion that the earth is flat.[50]

Yet who measures sanity levels? Secular man?

Part Two

THE CHRISTIAN PERSON

Ah, we who still call ourselves Christians are from the Christian point of view so pampered, so far from being what Christianity does indeed require of those who want to call themselves Christians, dead to the world, that we hardly ever have any idea of that kind of earnestness.

—Søren Kierkegaard

MENTORED AND DISCIPLED FOR CHRISTIAN LIVING

We have up to now examined three models of mentoring: the Heroic, the Stoic, and the Therapeutic. As we reflect upon these three distinct levels of mentoring, we may interpret them as representative of the developmental stages of our lives, as they have also been of the history of selfhood. When we create an absolute out of one aspect of reality, we create heresy, that is, a falsification of reality. To be sensitive is to use our senses; to be sensual is to be absorbed only with our own and other people's bodies. To be virtuous is to be aware of the need of a wholesome moral life; to be moralistic is to make moralism an end in itself. Likewise, to be healthy, mentally as well as bodily so, is appropriate; but to assume that emotional health is all the health we need may be a fatal flaw.

This is the heresy of all "isms," that they make absolute only certain aspects of the fullness of life before God, our

Maker. Now we will further explore the three models of mentoring, interpreting them as stages of human consciousness, which is how Søren Kierkegaard (1813–1855) interpreted them. So he will lead us, as our mentor, in this critique.

STAGES ON LIFE'S WAY

In childhood and youth, we live more sensately, immediately; we "enjoy life as it comes." It is a stage where our external environment is compelling and where we adjust constantly to its vicissitudes. However, as our social horizons expand in young adulthood, we may become more conscious of other people in our lives and be challenged to live more morally responsible to ourselves and for others, to the point we may embrace a major ideal or cause. Later still is a time to review the whole narrative of our lives, seeking to "make sense of it all" and to find therapeutic health and help from the guidance of other significant people in our lives.

We can, however, remain fixated at any one stage. Clearly Odysseus (Ulysses)—or his literary counterparts such as Don Juan and James Bond—did. The Stoic's quest for the virtuous life may stagnate at the stage of remaining merely moralistic. The therapeutic stage our culture has reached for, to free and expand us, can also end up leaving us more dependent upon our therapist, as well as upon the cultural norms it induces us to accept uncritically.

Self-reflection is a necessary element to move forward beyond all these stages. Without it, we will be condemned to live "stuck lives." Certainly, it is the nature of the first stage to have little or no self-reflection; otherwise, one would no longer be caught up by the immediacy of the moment, to live sensuously or even in bondage to addictions.

More Stoic Than Christian

However, the decision to choose how one should live,

between reality and ideals, provides a more purposeful life, which gains more stability when it is habituated by disciplines, as indeed the Stoics cultivated the virtuous life. But even Christians can be more Stoic than Christian when the whole emphasis is upon "spiritual disciplines" as such, rather than upon the relationship we are privileged to enter into with God, by grace in Christ through His Spirit. Ideals can become then "the real" by rational decisions and repetitive acts. However, the more we enter into the moral realm without God's grace, the more also we need to promote moral strategies, to cope with guilt, to maintain consistency, and to reduce the extent to which passions may dominate us. Even non-Christian love itself may have to be eliminated, as the Stoics realized, because of its own deep ambiguities.[1]

Thus the moral pursuit in itself may end up as being too theoretical, suitable perhaps for the philosopher but not for everyday living. For only when "thought" is presumed to be "reality" can "virtue" become "realized." But the more honest one is with oneself, the more desire is engendered for wholeness of being to lead one out of an abstract world into a much more complex world of other people and of intimacy with one's self-understanding. Perhaps also the awareness of God leads one to live with much more mystery than a rational explanation can ever provide.

KIERKEGAARD AS A RELIABLE MENTOR

It is the remarkable genius of Kierkegaard that he recognized and depicted these stages of human consciousness, and indeed much more. He distinguished them as the Aesthetic, the Moral, and the Religious categories of selfhood, linking them with differing categories of "despair," or "sin," a malady affecting all dimensions of the self. He distinguished them, in turn, from the mysterious gift of becoming a Christian. He interpreted the essential human condition as the failure to be the self one truly is, a failure he had experienced personally within his own family. So he could write of these stages of selfhood, or life-periods or life-views (terms he used interchangeably), from the personal struggles of his own experiences.

Testimonies to Kierkegaard

Georg Brandes, a friend of Friedrich Nietzsche, wrote in 1881 that Kierkegaard was "one of the most profound psychologists who ever lived," a thinker who at his death left about thirty printed volumes (written during the last twelve years of his life), "which taken together constitute a literature within literature."[2] Reinhold Niebuhr echoed this, saying, "Kierkegaard is the profoundest interpreter of the psychology of the religious life ... since Augustine."[3] Ludwig Wittgenstein, one of the most influential shapers of contemporary thought, rated him as "the greatest thinker of the nineteenth century,"[4] even though it was the century of Kant, Hegel, and Nietzsche.

Yet Kierkegaard was unknown outside of Denmark during his lifetime, and his works have often been (and even now are) misunderstood. Perhaps, argues the psychiatrist O. Hobart Mowrer, "Freud had to live and write before the earlier work of Kierkegaard could be carefully understood and appreciated."[5]

Kierkegaard's Attack on Idealism

What all three models of mentoring we have described have in common, and which we now find Kierkegaard had already identified clearly, is the primary role reason has always played in Western consciousness, even to the extent that "thought" is assumed the equivalence of "reality." This assumption, as we have seen, is markedly evident in Stoicism as well as in some schools of modern therapy. Yet as a theological student, aged twenty-two, desultory and without direction, "theological thought" had done nothing for Kierkegaard. So he confessed in an intimate letter to a brother-in-law:

> What I really need is to get clear about *what I must do,* not what I must know, except insofar as knowledge must precede every action. What matters is to find a purpose, to see what it really is what God wills what I should do; the crucial thing is to find the truth which is truth for me, to find *the idea for which I am to live and die.... This is what I need to lead a completely human life, and not merely one of knowledge.... This is what I need and this is what I strive for.*[6]
>
> (Emphasis added.)

A unity between the self as knower and doer, of theory and practice, is necessary, observed Kierkegaard, otherwise there is no unity within the self. This is what he meant when he frequently affirmed, "Truth is subjectivity." This is not the advocacy of subjectivism and the denial of objective canons for an advocacy of sheer feelings.[7] Nor is it objectivism as the abstraction, for example, of Hegelian idealism—Hegel being the philosopher Kierkegaard most attacked in this regard. Rather it is communicating the truth appropriately and personally. In simple terms, it is "practicing what you preach"! It is acknowledging there is no meaningful thought without action.

In humility, however, Kierkegaard saw himself only as a Christian "poet," meaning that he fell far short of the actuality of being a true Christian. Yet like other Christians he was striving toward that true end. Yes, his calling was to be a "witness to the truth" by devoting all his life's energies toward that intent. For he recognized strongly, "Christ did not teach that there was redemption for human beings, but he *redeemed* human beings" (emphasis added).[8] The gospel is not merely about a series of ideas that theologians write about; it is an event. We only "know" about it truly when we have participated in and through that event—as participants indeed, not just spectators.

RELIGION B, OR REAL CHRISIANITY

This is what Christian mentoring is all about—not the aesthetic, nor the Stoic, nor the psychoanalytic, nor any other religious models, but what Kierkegaard called "Religion B." By this he meant the unique consequences *actualized by the personal encounter with, and the response to, Jesus Christ.* He said: "Christ did not establish any doctrine ... he acted." And again: "Christian dogmatics ... must grow out of Christ's activity."[9]

In this, Kierkegaard was not anti-intellectual, as some have charged him. But he was against all intellectualism that would be obstacles to self-reflection or would substitute thought for reality. No valid mentor can be merely a theorist; one must communicate the "how," rather than the "what," of living wisely. Kierkegaard was equally concerned with the cure of diseases of the mind and emotions that handicap living fully. So his therapy was about unlearning old, destructive patterns and habits of thought, of confronting illusions and disentangling meanings, to appraise how we actually behave and live as *one* reality.[10]

THE SELF AS A RELATIONAL BEING

A related insight Kierkegaard gained from personal self-understanding was that the self is intrinsically relational. But in contrast to the Socratic quest, "Know thyself," self-identity in his day was being taken for granted, either in Romanticism, which simply assumed one discovered one's uniqueness, or in the Hegelian assumption that one just discovered intellectually the self-unfolding of Absolute Spirit. So Kierkegaard asked himself, "What is the self?" He found five qualifications were needed to answer this vital question:

> 1. The self is a relation.
> 2. The self is a relation that relates to itself.
> 3. The self, as a relation that relates to itself, is established in another, and in relating to itself relates to this other.
> 4. The self, as a relation, fails to relate to itself and therefore fails to relate to the other, and so finds itself in a dual disrelation of despair.
> 5. The self finds its despair only completely rooted out and healed when the self rests transparently in God who created the self.[11]

These qualifications set the direction for all his subsequent works, and indeed his own life journey. They are the key to understanding all his skills as a mentor. But first, let us explain *how* he can mentor us, before we describe what he will say to us.

KIERKEGAARD'S WAY OF MENTORING

Kierkegaard admitted he possessed no authority in living the Christian life. He was only a "poet." Modesty should always mark our so-called expertise in advising others how to live and relate to others. He took on, then, a Socratic or *maieutic* role. Just as a midwife helps to deliver at a birth, so we may facilitate new insights for others in the role of mentoring, but they must belong to the mentee in the first place. Kierkegaard helps us to gain insights about truthful existence. But the stress must be on the reader to gain these insights personally and appropriately so, just as it is the mother not the midwife who actually gives birth to the child. The mentor must then communicate in an indirect form of communication. Such a method may be unfamiliar to those of moderns who live according to self-help manuals and technical instructions about "how to fix things," including all our relationships (this usually means they remain permanently "unfixed"!).

His Use of Paradigmatic Characters

Kierkegaard did this by setting up paradigmatic characters. These were representative of various stages and positions of our own self-identifying roles and stages of selfhood, to portray relationally who and where we are. Some are authorial pseudonyms (like John Climacus); others are literary figures (such as Don Juan and Faustus); and still others are people we meet in our own world as concrete types of selfhood (such as Judge William, Vigilius Haufniensis, Constantine Constantius). They all represent various illusions we may have as the readers, mirroring back to us in self-reflection to elicit insight about our own state of consciousness. Kierkegaard used this device to protest against being surfeited with further "factual knowledge about" Christianity. For in his Danish culture, many were being deluged with religious information that kept them unaware of how shallow they really were. We are following a similar device in this book, of showing how we all live "influenced" (if not deliberately "mentored" lives), as lives shaped by associates and authors around us.

Kierkegaard wants to show us that we need to develop capacities for living the truth, which requires communicating more deeply in a context of life than, say, listening to a three-point sermon. The truth can be transforming. To see where we actually are in the stages of life's way helps us map out the situation of our own hearts in relating to ourselves, to others, and especially to God. As Kierkegaard put it: "Nearsighted people do not believe that others some distance away can see them. Likewise, the nearsighted sinner does not believe that God sees his straying."[12]

So a writer communicates through the life-views of such "nearsighted" characters to expose us as readers, indeed, in all our inadequate attempts to be real human beings. Some of these authors are more pseudo than others, depending on how far they are from reality. Thus this "second authorship" is a powerful, didactic form of mentoring, which hides the author in order to remove any "authorial dogmatism"—"tyranny" is what Kierkegaard calls it. It is a foolish therapist who insists, "You cannot be my client unless you follow exactly my school of therapy," as if merely having the right know-how is the remedy. Wisdom is subtler and therefore more indirect in communicating and eliciting the truth. So we have learned the value of case studies: "Take the case of so-and-so, and see what actually happened. Would you want to do the same?"

Thus case studies were presented by Kierkegaard to express the diversity and full context of life, not just abstract ideas or even doctrines. Communicating about living is a multilayered task, because processing data alone overlooks the needed capacities for living such realities. Faith, hope, and love remain concepts unless the capacities to trust, to hope, and to receive and share love are recognized and also provided for. Indeed, the simple task is merely being a writer. The real challenge is the difficult task of *being the truthful reader,* which requires both "heart" and "head" to apply the truth wholly to one's entire life.

His Use of the Bible

Kierkegaard also immersed the reader in the biblical narrative, which he interpreted as the grammar of the

Christian life, rather as a lover is immersed in a beloved's letters.

> Would it ever occur to the lover to read a letter from his beloved with a commentary? While reading the letter you are occupied with yourself and your relation to the beloved, but you are not objectively occupied with the beloved's letter, that this passage may be interpreted in ten ways—ah no, the important thing for you is to begin to act as soon as possible.[13]

Therapists, especially those engaged heavily in psychoanalysis, may be described as "soul archaeologists" who leave no stone unturned to reach "rock bottom." This was the issue of Jung's quarrel with Freud—why Freud refused so resolutely to accept the reality of the religious dimension of human existence. Freud was afraid of Jung's Gnostic curiosity and especially of his involvement with the occult, calling it an "obsessional neurosis." Both ended in seeking to suppress religion as historically developed, although in contrasted ways: Freud by suppression, and Jung by obsession with a form of universal Gnosticism. Today, however, the more popular adoption of relationally oriented models of therapy (such as object relations theory) has enabled some recovery of interest in religion—or at least less suppression—within psychotherapy.[14]

With Kierkegaard, the mystery of the human self, created in the image of God, was too deep to allow any suppression. The ideal for human life is transparency, which he described this way: "In relating to itself and in willing to be itself, the self rests transparently in the power that established itself,"[15] that is, in God. Kierkegaard pushes us to explore as far as we can go, never allowing us to exercise what Freud called the "dynamic unconsciousness," which is another name for either conscious suppression or unconscious repression. Instead, he took self-deception far more radically than Freud ever could, for he saw it is biblical to be associated with sin and despair as the universal condition of humanity.

His Christian Humility as True Realism

While we may be tempted to call him a genius, Kierkegaard has a contrary perspective. "A genius is nature's extraordinary," he observes, "no man being able to make himself a genius, whereas a Christian is freedom's extraordinary, or more properly, freedom's ordinary ... [this] is what everyone ought to be."[16] By this, Kierkegaard meant that the genius is self-grounded, whereas the true Christian is freed from being self-grounded, in sharpest contrast to the self-based models Heroic, Stoic, or secular Therapeutic mentors. Indeed, his category of the "demonic" is on a continuum of this, namely of having an absolute relationship to oneself that is even held onto in hell!

This estrangement between the Christian and these classical (also contemporary) models of mentoring is not an ideological construct—as philosophers and psychologists tend to argue (indeed as Hegel, Kierkegaard's archenemy, voiced). Rather, it is the gulf between abstraction and what is specifically relational and personal. Should we not all realize that human sciences only rationalize after the facts? They cannot redeem the past, nor can they actualize love in the present, nor even give hope for the future.

Unreal Role of the Therapist

But Kierkegaard saw himself as representative of the human condition in intimate realism. He helps us see how unreal is the role of the therapist: It is an intensive series of sessions, not an ongoing, day-to-day relatedness; it is a

paid friendship; it is primarily nonjudgmental in acceptance; it may be a substitute for the inadequacies of
parenting; and it is often the transference of the client's
expectations upon the therapist. But suppose the client
were to have an affair with the therapist's spouse; then we
would expect raw reactions in such a real-life situation to
become very different indeed! Would the therapist then
continue to be as clinically detached, nonjudgmental, and
accepting as before?

In contrast, Kierkegaard was a realist who had experienced personally the depths of despair, anxiety, and
the reality of sin. Yet he had not been overwhelmed by
them. He understood that a universal diagnosis was
essential for an individual remedy. Realistically he saw
that to be a real Christian, we all need to relate truly to
ourselves as well as to God. But the cure for the human
condition is faith in God: "Faith is: that the self in being
itself and willing to be itself rests transparently in
God."17

KIERKEGAARD'S VIEW OF
UNCONSCIOUSNESS, DESPAIR, AND SIN

Kierkegaard belonged to that long tradition of Christian
anthropology that teaches there is no knowledge of the
self without the knowledge of God. To "know thyself" is
not enough. It assumes too much self-ability, even with
the modesty Plato and others assumed was necessary for
this task. Such an assumption is dynamic unconsciousness: "what I choose not to recognize, or intentionally fail
to perceive," observes C. Stephen Evans.18 Legitimately, we
may be unaware of our internal physical behavior as
"unnoticed unconsciousness." But the dynamic unconscious is surely the part of oneself which one actively
resists confronting—perhaps because it is too painful

emotionally to face—or resists knowing for a multitude of reasons.

But Kierkegaard's strong intent was to see "the truth as inwardness," precisely because his own father could never face his own guilt and despair. He saw the majority of the human race practicing the same thing every day of their lives, like serfs who live on a feudal estate, unaware of being participants in a hierarchical social abstraction called feudalism. He recognized the period he was living in as the beginning of the modernization in Denmark and the formation of the modern Danish self. It was one in which the new abstraction of a democratic state and its culture were replacing the reality of God,[19] even though the Danish people still thought of themselves as being "religious"—as postmoderns now see themselves as "spiritual."

Human Beings Are Essentially Relational

We return then to Kierkegaard's basic question: "What is the self?" By saying the self is a relation, he was asserting there is an indissoluble duality or polarity within the human condition, as well as a synthesis as a relation between the two. These he expressed as "the temporal and the eternal"; "infinitude and finitude"; "freedom and necessity." Yet it is not the relation itself that constitutes the self, but the unity between the two acts of relating "to oneself" and "to the other" that are inseparable. The "other" is ultimately God.

Human beings by themselves fail to achieve such harmonious inner unity. The lack of it is what Kierkegaard calls "despair." This comes from within the self and from the failure to have freedom. "There is not a single human being," observed Kierkegaard, "who does not ... secretly harbor an unrest, an inner strife, a disharmony, an angst about an unknown something ... an angst about oneself ...

no human being ever lived who has not despaired."[20] We can be quite smug about what we estimate to be our successes in life, until we reckon on our relationships. Nowhere do we recognize a greater sense of failure than in how we relate to other people. How much more so, when we reflect upon our relations with God, do we know failure? Here then, observes Kierkegaard, is where there is the universal failure or despair, which he interprets as sin before God.

Do Men and Women Sin Differently?

Modern feminists have questioned whether there are not distinctively feminine and masculine ways of sinning, the one more recessive and negative of one's identity, the other more assertive and willful.[21] Kierkegaard not only allows for such distinctive types, but recognizes also a common human nature to both sexes. Making choices that eternally matter is how one can become truly a self. This is the core of the teaching of Kierkegaard, for the self is not "a thing" but a way of being. Hence it can be healthy or in sickness, in freedom or in necessity. But being created by God, being a derived relation, means that if I am to live as a true self, male or female, I must do so in relation to God.

Very real differences as men and women are allowed for by Kierkegaard, but it is *how* we choose to be a self before God that is crucial.[22] For we want naturally to get lost in the crowd, to become "mass man" or "mass woman," a copy, a number, and we despair in the loss of self. To be a self before our Creator and indeed our Redeemer is beyond our own desires or capabilities without response to God's love. But as God reveals His love to us, giving us space "to be," so the task and joy of human life is to understand, affirm, and love the other as *other*, whether male or female.

Sin as Despair

Kierkegaard's father first observed of his son that "he lived in quiet despair," and yet "he never questioned him more closely—alas, he could not, for he, too, lived in quiet despair." Neither one could help the other. Later Kierkegaard learned within himself that despair really "means to lose the eternal."[23] Just as dizziness is a composite of the psychical and the physical, so in all despair "there is the interplay of finitude and infinitude, of the divine and the human, of freedom and necessity."[24] So he summed all the categories of despair as follows:

> To despair over oneself, in despair to will to be
> oneself, in despair to be rid of oneself, in despair
> to will to devour oneself is the formula for all
> despair, to which also the other form of despair, in
> despair to will to be oneself, can be traced back,
> just as the above, in the despair not to will oneself,
> to will to be rid of oneself, is traced back to: in
> despair to will to be oneself.[25]

The density of such language is comparable to the ways Kierkegaard also outlined the relationships of which the self consists, discussed above. We need then to outline the ways Kierkegaard interprets our attempts to gain personal unity, unreal and real.

WAYS OF BEING UNREAL INDIVIDUALS AS STAGES OF CONSCIOUSNESS

Kierkegaard helps us to see more clearly how falsifying are the forms of mentoring we have discussed in our first three models of mentoring. We will look at his Aesthetic state of consciousness, Ethical stage of consciousness, and Religion A.

The Aesthetic Stage of Consciousness

What we have called the Heroic, he called the Aesthetic Self. He described it indirectly in *Either/Or*. It is a way of being that is characterized by deeply rooted tensions and contradictions within itself, as the self oscillates between enthusiasms and dread. It is expressive of "finite's despair," in worldliness, sensationalism, pragmatism, and yet also in paralyzed restlessness. It is sensately always on the move to the next novelty or project.

Quite simply, Kierkegaard saw the first task for every human being is to become a self, as the "third" entity beyond the polarities of body/soul, finite and infinite, necessity/possibility. It is in coming to consciousness that one becomes a self and thus can enter into self-consciousness. It occurs when the dreamer begins to "do" something and to actualize his or her existence. It is like Ulysses returning home to Penelope and Telemachus, now ready to face his responsibilities for the first time. It is depicted in the parable of the prodigal son, now remembering his prior existence, ready to remove himself from the swine trough to go back home to the Father.

This decision can be costly—Kierkegaard used the word "angst" to describe it—as "a desire for what one fears, a sympathetic antipathy."[26] It is the kind of action taken when an addict breaks away from the addiction. Indeed it is a continuing struggle throughout each stage of living, for whatever is a possibility leaves us with a shadowy existence we may despair of ever being realized. Yet freedom beckons us to rise above being merely animal in existence. "Freedom" means both "the possibility" beyond us and "the choice" we make. So we are encouraged to reflect as the first step toward self-consciousness.

But Kierkegaard contended that "most people virtually never advance beyond what they were in their childhood and youth: immediacy with the admixture of a little dash of reflection."[27] He says, "The whole question of the self becomes, in a deeper sense, a kind of blind door in the background of one's soul, behind which there is nothing." Becoming oneself requires then the shattering of this sensate, immediate self to welcome the angst as a friend, not an enemy, in order to recognize the radical difference between one's finiteness and one's infinitude.

The Ethical Stage of Consciousness

The second, or Ethical, stage of consciousness or form of existence comes then with the radical break from the antecedent condition, to live qualitatively on a different basis. As his character Judge William observes:

> There comes a moment in a man's life when his immediacy is, as it were, ripened and the spirit demands a higher form in which it will apprehend itself as spirit. Man, so long as he is immediate spirit, coheres with the whole earthly life, and now the spirit would collect itself, as it were, out of this dispersion and become in itself transformed, the personality would be conscious of itself in its eternal validity.[28]

As ideals are measured against reality, the result becomes the project of objective knowledge, which we have described as the character of the classical school of antiquity, notably Stoicism.

Kierkegaard saw Socrates as the perfect example of this Ethical stage. He used irony—in saying the opposite of what is meant—to help to loosen hearers from their attachments to the Aesthetic stage and to the immediacy of their existence, as determined by desire, talent, natural bent, and mood. Instead they are challenged and moved toward higher ethical ideals. Plato, however, was condemned by Kierkegaard as trying fantastically to rid himself of his actuality in his contemplation of the eternal. But the more realistic moral therapy of the Stoics is that they choose not immediacy but themselves. Their despair, while as universal as that of the Aesthetic Self, is different. It is not inflicted but chosen and actively willed as duty, discipline, obedience. Instead of living in flux, the ethical (Stoic) self is a historical unity, living and reliving attempts to live ethically.

In fact, Judge William recognizes that the Aesthetic Self is not really eliminated; it is harmoniously included in Ethical existence. He sees this illustrated in marriage, which may begin with the Aesthetic in the sensual attraction the parties have one for the other. Then the marriage is further sustained in moving into the Ethical level of existence toward each other. But unlike the Stoics, Judge William is also aware of a God-relationship. Is not marriage preferably performed in a church? he asks. Even though bias may be given to one's positive role in developing oneself (let alone within a marriage), yet the fear lurks of the inability of the self to be able to integrate itself without some authority figure lurking in the background. The disparity between what is and what ought to be is always there. Thus God remains a limited figure, assumed to be "there," in some "cooperative way, even if it is only as a cliché that 'God helps those who help themselves.'" More bluntly Kierkegaard directly said:

> The whole of existence of the human race rounds itself off as a perfect, self-contained sphere, and then the ethical is that which limits and fills at one and the same time. God comes to an invisible vanishing point, an impotent thought; his power is only in the ethical, which fills all existence.[29]

Nominal Religious Consciousness

The third level of the self, Religion A, is represented by Kierkegaard's next paradigm character, Johannes de Silentio. The "thought" of an absolute God challenges de Silentio to be superficially religious. God's transcendence shatters the immediacy on which the Ethical individual depends. The moral laws now become more demanding than the self-sustaining self can resist. The unavoidable failure begins when the self posits "an absolute relationship to the absolute," inviting the possibility of unity as a religious self. It is analogous to the unity of the self that the therapist promises in becoming the therapeutic self.

Becoming aware of the transcendence of God is so radically different from past existence, it requires an irrevocable severance with the past, as is often exhibited today in divorce, severance from one's parents, or in traumatic events and other "passages" now being advocated as necessary for one's pursuit of individual freedom. But if the idea of an absolute God still haunts one, as it did for another paradigm character, Johannes Climacus, the religious self is finally forced to admit its total inability to meet the divine demands and to face an increasing sense of guilt, and thus of an absolute distance from God. Any repentance, however, is like an army defeated in battle—having "lost the reins of government, ... it has only retained the power to grieve."[30] In other words, "repentance has gone crazy." Instead of the religious self becoming repentant toward God, it is turned even more internally within the self. Anxiety has now become identified with sin, but the self still questions how one can make one's own atonement for its condition. Here is where the therapist has no remedy, other than not to take "sin" so seriously.

This is well illustrated in T. S. Eliot's play *The Cocktail Party*, where Celia is a patient in the psychiatrist's clinic.

She describes her two symptoms of distress, hoping that they are personally her own, for if the whole world also has them, then "that's more frightening! That would be terrible." The first is "awareness of solitude ... that I've always been alone. That one always is alone." The psychiatrist asks about the second symptom. "It sounds ridiculous—but the only word for it that I can find, is a sense of sin ... and I don't feel as if I were: in fact, aren't the people one thinks of as immoral just the people who have no moral sense?" So Celia continues:

> It's not the feeling of anything I have ever *done,*
> which I might get away from, or anything in me I
> could get rid of—but of emptiness, of failure,
> towards someone, or something, outside of myself;
> and I feel I must ... *atone*—is that the word? Can
> you treat a patient for such a state of mind?[31]

Obviously, the psychiatrist can give only platitudes. Kierkegaard responded more bluntly when he concluded, "As soon as psychology has finished with anxiety, it is delivered to dogmatics."[32] Celia's malaise has become a theological issue.

True Christian Consciousness

Religion B, or vital Christian faith, begins theologically, states the character Anti-Climacus when any individual faces the "offense" that each one of us "exists before God." Indeed, this demands that each one of us should "live on the most intimate terms with God."[33] This we cannot do without God's most intimate and gracious help. Intrinsically, then, I find myself to be a failure before God—something much more radical than Celia was prepared to face. Resolution lies only in acceptance of God's Spirit, deep within oneself.

To do so, Kierkegaard admonishes, "Take Holy Scripture and lock your room," for "the person who is not alone with God's Word is not reading God's Word."[34] Then looking into it as in a mirror, one is led to intense personal conviction and repentance. He wrote: "For if God's Word is for you merely a doctrine, something impersonal, then it is no mirror ... it takes an authentic person, an 'I,' to look at oneself in a mirror." Forgiveness of sin then becomes not a mere declaration but the establishment of a living, working, continuing relationship that binds my spirit with God's Spirit, to become indeed a new self![35]

For Kierkegaard, then, the Christian life consists of new stages on life's way, indeed of a new existence. For one is now impacted by the Spirit of God within oneself to live anew in the way of faith in, hope for, and love of God.

KIERKEGAARD'S PATHOLOGY OF
DESPAIR AND THE UNCONSCIOUS

While becoming a Christian is personally responding to Christ's love in faith, Kierkegaard diagnosed that the deepest mystery is that, when the self is confronted by and offered God's love, it instead withdraws into itself. Then indeed it suffers "the sickness unto death." Yet Kierkegaard's main purpose in all his writings is to communicate hope that lies by faith in love, which is "willing to be itself and to rest transparently in the power (i.e., God) that established it."[36]

As he said in *The Sickness unto Death* (1849), one of his finest works: "Everything essentially Christian must have as its presentation a resemblance to the way a physician speaks at the sickbed; even if only medical experts understand it, it must never be forgotten that the situation is the bedside of a sick person."[37] But take note that Kierkegaard's understanding of sickness is wholly incompatible with that of

Freud's. It is despair as ultimately the human condition of sin—of humankind's condition before the Infinite, in the sight of God our Creator. Thus it is relational pathology—not sexual repression or other neuroses. Secular therapists can have no categories to explore the depth to which Kierkegaard identified this basic and universal deficiency of God-relatedness. This relational pathology, in turn, creates imbalance among all the components of the self as an inner synthesis before God.[38]

Types of Despair

In the attempt to synthesize infinite and finite without faith, despair is the consequent dark shadow, since it becomes a misrelation.[39] For in exploring distinct categories of despair, Kierkegaard wanted to demonstrate forcefully the intrinsic insufficiency of an unaided self-relatedness. Human beings cannot rely upon themselves to gain their freedom.

Infinite's despair is a state in which the self becomes sentimental without reality in sheer proliferation of objective knowledge perhaps or in fantastic "projects." *Finite's despair* is characterized by living sensately, in worldliness, in conformity, or in a merely pragmatic, prudential view of life. *The synthesis of the temporal and eternal* likewise creates inherent tensions, such as between the self's capacity for unity through time and its tendency toward dispersion in different moments, and lacking the unifying meaning of all one's life, as God alone knows us. Yet without the omniscience, we tend to abstract our life and thus to stultify it. But the despair of this distance between the temporal and the eternal forced Kierkegaard to make a confession that strikes a chord with many today: "My life is absolutely meaningless." Likewise, *possibility's despair* is fascination with possibility in itself. But *necessity's despair,* on the other hand, involves the lack of possibility, a kind of fatalism or narrowness of life. All these aspects of despair are expressive of the aesthetic context of human experience, that is, preoccupation with the senses.

In contrast, it was observed of Nicholas Herman of Lorraine (affectionately known as Brother Lawrence) that "in the greatest hurry of business in the kitchen he still preserved his recollection and heavenly mindedness." That is to say, being a Christian—not just an aesthete—he was able to synthesize the temporal and the eternal within himself. So the time of kitchen work and the attitude of prayer become interpreted as one.[40]

The self, as self-relating and upbuilding, belongs to the Ethical dimension of selfhood. Here despair is related to self-consciousness in self-love, self-hate, and self-judgment, self-direction, and so on. Here despair takes on "higher forms," for it is much more self-related. Kierkegaard spoke first of *despair in weakness,* where the self is unwilling to be itself, that is, in will-lessness. The second is *in despair to will to be oneself,* that is, in defiance, or willfulness. It is not then a true relatedness either way, because it is not willing to enter into relational responsiveness.

This leads then to the third, or religious, level of humankind's need of further unity, to be dependent entirely upon God.[41] This is not that God is merely man's wishful projection of need as Feuerbach, and later Freud, interpreted it. For God reveals Himself personally in many ways: as Creator, Judge, and Redeemer. Here our inadequacy to relate to God as seen in Religion A is indeed "the despair of sin." The sickness that was first conceived to be psychological, then to be ethical, is now seen to be sinful rebellion and disobedience of the Creator. For God is both our criterion and goal, so that the more transparent persons we become, the more sinful we realize we are; and the more our relationship to Christ grows, the more awareness of sin is intensified. The response can only be either of despairing resignation or of repentant faith.

Despair Unconscious as Well as Conscious

Kierkegaard's ideal for human life is primarily transparency before God and therefore self-understanding in knowing God. In this interpretation the "dynamic unconscious" of Freud is far more than being pathological; it is sinful indeed![42] For the dynamic unconscious is that part of me I do not want to know nor to allow God to confront me with. For this unconscious is what I intentionally do not want to perceive or to allow to be examined. As we all know, a "facade of normalcy" or of being "well adjusted" can mask what is seriously damaged below the surface of our lives. Puritans like John Owen were well aware that sin goes hand in hand with self-deception.[43] Kierkegaard can speak then of the "despairing unconsciousness of God" as "not being in despair, not being conscious of being in despair." This he argues "is precisely a form of despair." But there is a distinction also between the personal consciousness of God and the universal consciousness of God, as God in His revealed character. So to be "religious" in the sense of having a consciousness of the existence of God is not to be confused with being a "Christian," as being related personally with God.

The Cure of Faith

To summarize briefly, Kierkegaard interprets the unconscious as something one promotes by self-deception about who or what one is. It may be laziness or the inertia of everyday life that promotes it, or the narcotic of busyness that stultifies. Or worst of all, it can be intensified sinisterly by pride, that is, the refusal to submit oneself as a creature before God. So pride can lead us to play the role of making ourselves God substitutes.

Humanly speaking, there is no psychological therapy that can ever remove such falsification, because it involves our own specific relationship before God. The cure for this human condition can only be faith in God. Faith, then, says Kierkegaard, "is that the self in being itself, and in willing to be itself, rests transparently in God."[44] Such a faith means that the dynamic unconscious within me, which because of sin I cannot and will not recognize, has been removed, indeed blotted out. For I would know myself, even as I am known of God.

Such Christian transparency in God is the cure for despair. Yet despair is a necessary experience to have in order to be challenged to live at a higher level of existence than one naturally lives with. Indeed, the progress of faith is related to the deepening consciousness of sin. Kierkegaard saw that the opposite of sin is not virtue, but faith. Indeed, faith is the highest level of human existence, a new state of "being a self," for it is faith in Christ, the God-man, who makes it possible for the human being to live in God and no longer live autonomously. Appropriately, we conclude with one of Kierkegaard's own prayers:

> Father in heaven! What is a man without Thee!
> What is all that he knows, vast accumulation
> though it be, but a chipped fragment if he does
> not know Thee! What is all his striving, could it
> even encompass a world, but a half-finished work
> if he knows not Thee: Thee the One, who art one
> thing and who art all! So may Thou give to the
> intellect, wisdom to comprehend that one thing;
> to the heart, sincerity to receive this understand-
> ing; to the will, purity that wills only one thing.[45]

*Throughout the entire history of Western thought the equation
of the person with the thinking, self-conscious individual has led
to a culture in which the thinking individual has become the highest
concept in anthropology.... Love alone, free love, unqualified by natural necessities, can generate personhood.*[1]

—John D. Zizioulas

DISCIPLED TO BE
PERSONS IN CHRIST

In his essay "On Friendship," the skeptic Montaigne declares, "O friend, there is no friend!" He attributes this to Aristotle, although he lingers long upon Cicero's reflections on friendship too. Jacques Derrida, the modern-day "father of deconstruction," makes this statement the theme of his recent work *Politics of Friendship* (1997). Friendship can exist only between good men, Cicero insists. But who is good enough for the ideals of friendship? asks Derrida. Friendship with God may help us, argues Aristotle, except that He is so remote and inaccessible. Presence or proximity is the condition for friendship.[2] Moreover, God has no need of a friend. Why then should man ever come to believe he needs a friend or to make friendship a mark of being human?

For Derrida it is all a rational human formula:

> I think, therefore I am the other; I think, therefore I
> need the other (in order to think); I think, therefore
> the possibility of friendship is lodged in the move-
> ment of my thought in so far as it demands, calls
> for, desires the other, the necessity of the other, the
> cause of the other at the heart of the cogit.[3]

This is a parody on Descartes; nevertheless, it cannot wholly escape from his bias. For it ignores the Christian claim that love, not reason, is transcendent, hence the crucial importance of Zizioulas's statement above. Only love can generate personhood.

"Deconstruction" is a strategy for "undoing." The mind may be a mirror, but does it reflect upon reality or only upon itself? The abuse of authority and the use of power in claiming to know and speak the truth alarm deconstructionists. Not only priests who claim to have God on their side, but also philosophers who claim to know the truth are challenged. It is taking psychoanalysis a stage further: the rational questioning of both motive and intent of the therapist, and indeed of all professions. Derrida is an iconoclast of idols, without, however, being able to appreciate the contrast between the idol and the icon. So deconstructionism leaves us with indeterminacy about truth and reality, in lacking the personal dimension, that is, of not living before the personal God.

But it does something positive in deepening and extending the role played by hermeneutics, or human communication, to be much more than merely the interpretation of texts. Language is the serious business of being human, in all its mixed motives and all its needs within social life. For communication is much more than simply being rational about it, although we need to be that. Beyond the rational, all great Christian thinkers have seen the love of God. In contrast, not even deconstructionists can envisage beyond reason, other than to see anarchy. Indeed, without the love of God, we are incapable of moving outside the categories of the antimodels of mentoring we have been describing.

THE WESTERN QUEST FOR THE PERSONAL

Kierkegaard has already helped us to see that as a human being, I have a relationship of myself, to myself, within myself. I become two, subject and object, in need of self-recognition for self-affirming and also self-knowing.[4] Yet in such self-realization, I learn to see myself as other-dependent, as dependent on external realities I cannot control.

The Aesthetic or Heroic View of "Person"

This is evident in the child learning to be self-expressive and saying, "Look at me!" as we have seen represented in the Aesthetic or Heroic model. For the Greeks, the "person" is the *dramatis personae* of the stage. An actor dons a mask, through which the sound comes (literally *per sonare*) to act out the many roles he plays. His roles and place in the narrative devolve from the choices that place him in a dramatic role before others.[5] Behind this Greek word *prosopon* lies possibly the Etruscan *persu*, which may have reference to Persephone, the goddess of the underworld. So this idea of the "person" inevitably remains shadowy indeed![6] For in the Greek ordering of the cosmos, with its harmony of universals, there can be no ultimate place for particulars, such as a unique human being. The individual protest of a human being for freedom, within this sphere of abstract universals and rational necessity, is cause for much human tragedy, precisely because he can only remain impersonal.

Odysseus certainly has a "personality," as lusty as any

Greek hero could have! He fights with the gods, and such self-determination is at times even respected by them. Homer's world is populated with "personalities." Penelope can weep over her absent husband:

> How I long for my husband—alive in memory always,
> that great man whose fame resounds through
> Hellas right to the depths of Argos![7]

Yes, such self-actualizing, individualistic character is vividly depicted by the Greeks, whether by the tragedians Euripides or Sophocles, or by the philosophers Plato or Aristotle. What greater personality could there be than Socrates! But ultimately, a human being's individuality cannot be fitted into the "other-dependence," the universality of the cosmos, that ultimate harmony of the "all" into the "one."[8] When Socrates teaches, "Know thyself," he is merely reminding his disciples to remember to find and fit themselves into the total scheme of things with humility. It is folly to do or think other than this! No intellectual system since then has ever been able to account for you and me in our uniqueness within the general scheme of things "out there."[9] Thus the stream of individualistic self-analysis, now so intensified by the "therapeutic revolution," could have had no place within the Greek consciousness of personality.

The Stoic View of "Person"

The second stage of personhood occurs when self-enactment becomes more rational and accepting of external modes of moral life, as in a growing child "at school." The Stoics now gave a *theory* to the idea of personhood, because they inhabited a rational universe. They would argue we are endowed with reason to be moral, by which we can ascertain what is virtuous and dutiful for the universal moral ordering of our existence. This is Cicero's theory of "persons," of having the necessary legal sanctions as citizens of the Roman world to abide by the universal "laws of nature." Here he follows an earlier Stoic, Panaetius. The individual "personality" is only definable and permissible within the universal framework of Roman law.[10] So at first, even women and children, as well as slaves, were defined as "nonpersons," or noncitizens. The Roman tag: *Servus non habet personam* (the slave has no personhood) wiped out at a stroke one-fifth of the population of imperial Rome as incapable of entering social relationships with their masters. Thus the Roman persona was the privileged unit of legal and religious responsibilities and duties to the state and to the gods.

The later Western world has lived in the uneasy tensions of these two definitions of "the person." Where the paradigm of "persons" is actors who choose to flout their sensual roles within a cognitive, conventional, moral society, the actors are condemned as worldly, for "worldliness" consists of the ability to act out with aplomb and grace a great variety of roles, some of them at least unconventional. But when the paradigm for "persons" comes from canon law, rather than from the theater, ownership becomes inherent in the rights and powers of moral rational action. Mind then becomes the clearest, best "self," as it did in the Enlightenment, when the autonomous rational self—*res cognitans*—or "Cartesian self," develops a mind-body detachment and the outside world of other people becomes distant indeed. Thus Descartes defines the "personal" as expressive of self-consciousness, itself most intensified when one "thinks" most of all! Immanuel Kant (1724–1804) takes this further to affirm one is most personal when one is most rational and moral also. This must necessarily mean being turned in on oneself as a reflexive being, making external relations of secondary or even peripheral significance.

Today's Politicization of Personhood

Today is now the world where the legal rights of a fetus (is it a person or nonperson?), of feminists, of homosexuals, and of many others have become politicalized by new definitions of personhood. Philosophers, historians, anthropologists, and psychologists, all in this century, have continued to add their insights/confusions as to "the meaning of persons."[11] But of all the ongoing theories of human identity, that of the Stoic character has had the greatest persistence, simply because it is the one in which the psychological and physiological traits can be most closely linked within a rational explanation, as Freud pioneered. It provides a "natural" framework of rational habits that give shape, form, and continuity to being a "habituated self" that appears cognitively reinforcing. It gives little scope, however, for the contingency of the emotions, other than the sexual, in a more personalized world of self-transcendence.

"THE PROBLEM THAT HAS NO NAME": THE PERSONAL IN A WORLD OF ABSTRACTION

If "persons" need "persons" to become "persons," as a Xhosa proverb observes, then the processes toward abstraction in our Western world are negative forces that threaten to depersonalize humanity. C. S. Lewis warned us prophetically half a century ago about this outcome in his lectures in *The Abolition of Man.*[12] Just as Nazi abstractionism dealt with the "Jewish Question" in the Holocaust, is it too far-fetched to suggest that "the Question of the Personal" may still be threatened, to be dealt with "scientifically"?

No Foundation for a "Person"

This is already happening in the political redefinition of the family. When 1994 was designated the International Year of the Family, Dr. Jonathan Sacks, the chief rabbi of

Britain, called it instead "the Year That the Family Died." He marked symbolically the beginning of that year with the burial of a coffin marked "International Year of the Family."[13]

If secular man loses all metaphysical foundations for "the person" and fails to distinguish God from everything else, living in fact as if he or she were a god, then the practical understanding of the true reality of everything else, as well as of his or her identity, is lost too.[14] Anthony Giddens has clearly described the fragility of the self by the impacts being imposed upon it by late modernity.[15] Personality tests such as the Myers-Briggs can be insightful, but their misuse can also become alienating. For if I am simply known as an ESFP or an INTJ on the categories of "personalities," I am worse off than the treatment Homer would have given me! Becoming clinical about my own identity for the sake of psychological self-management is no advance on the Stoics, especially if I ever had the benefit of a worldly-wise mentor comparable to Cicero or Seneca.

So when Betty Friedan wrote her best seller *The Feminine Mystique* (1965), she disclosed her own inner yearning associated with "the problem that has no name."[16] For beyond her functional roles as a wife and a mother—or at least as defined so by society—her basic self-desire was "who, not just what, do I want to be?" It is similar to the question of a friend of mine in the highly specialized career of neurosurgery: "Have I been cheated by society?" To which I responded, "Is it you who have cheated yourself, and is it your grandchildren who are telling you so?" For, of course, professionalism and specialization are forms of abstraction that tend toward the reduction of the "personal."

Even such an empathic therapist as Carl Rogers, as he speaks of "how I became the person I am" in his book of essays, *On Becoming a Person,* can only describe the process of becoming a self-creating "individual"; so his title is wrong.[17] For it is all about "becoming an individual"! In fact, he tells us he rejected his parents' Christian faith to become "myself." Even his approval of Kierkegaard is misplaced, because he cannot appreciate Kierkegaard's Christian polemic. So Rogers has no ground upon which to differentiate the "person" from the "individual." In fact the "therapeutic self," argues Christopher Lasch, ends up as the "minimal self" in a culture of survivalism.[18]

In his essays, significantly named *The Inhuman*, Jean-François Lyotard explores the inhumanity of the institutions of modernity, as well as the ways in which the soul is held hostage within oneself by self-possessiveness.[19] These two types of "inhumanity"—of what society does to me to generate discontent and what I do to myself, hence my "despair" in Kierkegaard's term—are really both expressive of individualism. It is then that the misery of the small child becomes archetypal of the human condition as an "individual."

For shorn of speech, unable to stand upright, hesitating over the selection of objects to observe, unable to feed itself, unable to calculate for self-advantage, a child is vulnerable indeed without the social protection and support of parenting. Jesus uses this image of our need of God: "Unless you change and become like little children, you will never enter the kingdom of heaven."[20]

THE INDIVIDUAL AND THE PERSON

What Lyotard is calling "inhuman" is just that: the "individual," the inwardness of self-enclosure. But he is silent about its opposite, the "person."[21] This "person" represents the ecstatic posture of looking outward, finding identity and well-being in the Other, as the child does when the miracle of recognition occurs reciprocally in seeing the mother's face. The transformation that then takes place can only be described as "joy." Foundational then to personhood is what Ricoeur calls attestation,[22] that is, the credence and trust given to oneself by another. Childhood, then, should never be forgotten, for its needs illuminate what is essential in distinguishing between inhumanity and personhood as the genuinely human.

The following table may help us to distinguish this contrast between the "individual" of inhumanity and the "person" as the social reality of true humanness.[23]

THE INDIVIDUAL	THE PERSON
Secular anthropological understanding	Theological revelation (*imago Dei*)
Humans created in own image	Humans created in the image of God
Identity based on human action	"Made righteous" by God's justification
Freedom defined within the autonomous self	Freedom defined as self-transcendence, that is, from self-groundedness "in Christ"
Sin as self-enclosure, "unrighteous-ness" and disobedience	Discipleship as "openness to God," based upon His calling

The Reductionism of Science

Characteristic of scientific anthropology, the British *A Dictionary of the Social Sciences* has several articles on the "individual," but none on the "person."[24] When philosophers define the "person" as an ethical issue, they are distinguishing what is a human being from either a fetus or some other material concept.[25] The human person remains unresolved as a questionable issue, scientifically inaccessible, and indefinable. The human can only be a question mark. It is only in the theological analogy drawn between persons—human and divine—that theological anthropology beings to make sense in defining us as persons-in-relation-with-God.[26] For science and philosophy have only their own canons of defining humanness within their own restricted understandings, which are inevitably reductionistic and alienating. The mystery of humanity cannot be explored by them.

The *locus classicus* of theological anthropology is Genesis 1:26: "Then God said, 'Let us make man in our image, in our likeness.'" First, this tells us that God is the kind of God who has identified Himself irrevocably with humanity, in covenant love.[27] Without God, humanity is a mystery. But, likewise, without humanity God is unknowable. This amazes the psalmist, when in Psalm 8 he wonders why, of all Creator Yahweh's creatures, God should choose human beings as His covenant partners.

Second, "image" implies relationality, as "male and female created he them," in coequality and complementarity. Humanity is also given a mandate of stewardship over creation, to define further its God-given status, responsibility, and relationship with creation. This vertical relationship before God as His representative on earth continues even after the fall, although now the seriousness of sin is intensified by bearing the *imago Dei* in sinful "unlikeness." The incarnation, in which the human-intent-of-God is recapitulated in Christ, is now where the image and likeness of God is revealed in its final, eternal expression. True personhood now is in "being conformed to the icon and likeness of Christ," "who is the icon of the invisible God."

The Faber Homo, *or Made Righteous by God?*

The "individual" today, autonomous as the modern technocrat, becomes the measure of all things, with no sense of a stewardship given by God. The individual decides what will become of the world, as *faber homo,* the human maker, with no reference to the Creator. For he or she assumes one's own self is constituted by one's own actions. In the Reformation, observes Eberhard Jungel, this posture was flatly contradicted by Luther, who said: "The work which I do does not make me into the person I am; rather the person who I am makes the work."[28] He rejects Aristotle's *Nicomachean Ethics*, which says, "We become just by doing just acts." No, all I am as a person "made righteous" and "justified freely by His grace" is the act of God. A Christian person is primarily one who receives but does not "attain" merit. Indeed, as Fénelon has reminded us, I receive myself from the goodness of God.

Freedom is the fundamental desire of what it is to be human in modernity. But if it is freedom for the individual, what then of the revolutionary triad of "freedom, equality, and fraternity"? Obviously, the more there is in it for me, the less there is in it for you! So what is freedom for me may be oppression for you! Moreover, from what do I really want freedom? For what purpose—to be more of an individual? If freedom is for more self-determination, when do I begin to wonder when and how I may need deliverance from my own self-destructive instinct and addictions? Freedom, then, as self-constituted, begins to look very much like self-loss and self-bondage. There are too many ambiguities and contradictions embedded in "freedom as an individual."

The Christian gospel calls us to repentance in acknowledging the sinfulness and self-destructiveness of self-constituted freedom. Personal freedom lies in the "justified life," in which God acts on our behalf, in the humanity of Christ, so that "if the Son shall make you free, you are free indeed." As Christoph Schoebel has put it succinctly:

> The true measure of freedom is love as the relationship which makes the flourishing of the other the condition of self-fulfilment. Human freedom becomes the icon of divine freedom where the freedom of divine grace constitutes the grace of human freedom.[29]

It is freedom from the bondage of sin, freedom from self-groundedness, the freedom of the children of God.

PERSONHOOD DEMANDS CHRISTIAN DISCIPLESHIP

The call to discipleship, as the Gospels make clear, is Christ's initiative, not ours. It is an uncompromising demand to "leave everything and follow Me." This is definitive of becoming personally "like Christ." It thus transforms autonomy, to become "open" to the Other. It is self-renunciation. Allegiance to Christ means "self-abandonment," as French Christian writers like Fénelon emphasized strongly in the seventeenth century. Conformity to Christ thus reconstructs one's whole manner of "being" and "doing." So as Alistair McFadyen has aptly defined Christian discipleship, it is intrinsically, as well as extrinsically, "openness" to God, as putting one's whole life in a wholly new context; truly a new creation.[30] This is also vitally a renewed transparency of life, in which one's person is nurtured and grows in relationships.

God Is Our Goal

As we always remain incomplete in "becoming persons," this is also an eschatological orientation toward the future. For God now becomes our goal, or *telos;* it is no longer oneself. Yet our objective remains incomplete. Our true humanity is still unfinished. But the "person" is henceforth oriented toward a future destiny. "Not as though I have already attained," confesses the apostle, "but I seek after." For incorporated in God's *eschaton* is "newness" that is still to be unfolded and revealed. It is "new" in two ways: (1) we can never give or achieve it ourselves—it is of God alone; and (2) it is "new" in making the old "old," leaving it to perish.[31] "Therefore, if anyone is in Christ, he is a new creation; the old has gone, the new has come! All this is from God...."[32]

Constantly, we need to be reminded of this in our unbelief, for God is a revealing God, not a static monad but an ongoing initiator of love. Such language transcends, then, our own psychological language and our own self-analysis. For this divinely inspired "newness" brings redemptive transformation of our relationships "beyond all that we can ask or think," so we still "do not know what we shall be," admits the apostle, other than we shall be "like him."

The "person," then, is a self-abandoned, open category and thus is still an unfulfilled category of being. It has iconic existence, we have seen, because it is like being a window, looking out to the future of God's intent of love. To this we are "called." So to this we "respond," just as the first disciples heard the call of Jesus: "Follow Me." Distractedly, we are constantly being called by others and by other things as part of the hazard of our "openness." To live in the light of the eternal it is essential for us to know where we are going, that is, to know our "calling."

Confusion in the Church

Much confusion occurs today within the life of the church and of what is claimed to be "Christian," because Christians themselves do not distinguish these two categories: the individual and the person. "Discipleship" tends often to be about becoming a more efficient religious entrepreneur, even merchant, of the "gospel," certainly an activist. These are categories churches leaders do not challenge, because these are their roles. The cult of religious "leadership" is not examined to see how often it is narcissistic and not self-giving.

NEW TESTAMENT DISCIPLESHIP

With the advent of the person of Jesus Christ, a new human reality has entered the world. Being a member of

God's people in the Old Testament did link them to the "God of Abraham, Isaac, and Jacob," corporately and individually. Now an individuated faith takes on a new dimension, for it is "in Christ." It is expressed in the German world *individualitat,* which implies that individual realization is only possible in relation to a social whole.[33] It is often expressed in the Psalms, where the "I" of the psalmist may be both the personal as well as the corporate personality of Israel. But Paul's frequent phrase of being "in Christ" implies a whole new understanding of discipleship.

A common theme in classical education was the quest to become "godlike," for the pursuit of knowledge was the kind of activity in which the gods were assumed to be absorbed. It promised freedom, happiness, self-sufficiency, and self-control. But the New Testament writers speak instead of becoming "Christlike" or "in Christ," to become godly and pursue godliness.[34]

Christ's Discipleship

Five distinctions are evident in Christ's discipleship that contrast it from the classical or rabbinical schools. First, Christ's disciples do not choose Him, for it is His initiative to call them. Second, Jesus' call is inclusive, for all are sinners, and being ceremonially clean is not a category He accepts. Third, discipleship becomes now a radical reorientation of one's existence; it means "giving up all to 'follow Jesus.'" Fourth, it means sharing in the ministry of Jesus, to heal the sick, to give to the poor, and to live in the light of God's kingdom. Finally, it is above all expressive of Christ's love—suffering and loving as He does for us.[35]

In the Gospels, because Christian discipleship is so radical and comprehensive, it can only be described by diverse witnesses as multifaceted. A negative presentation is given in Mark to warn the reader that without the passion of Christ, discipleship will be wholly misunderstood.[36] In

Matthew, "making disciples" suggests that personal relationship with Christ means much more than merely being "taught."[37] For Luke it is the everydayness of discipleship, living caringly with the poor, the sick, and the afflicted. Yet it is also mysteriously "carrying our cross." "Following Jesus" also entails being with Him throughout the whole world, spreading the gospel as the Acts of the Apostles record what actually happened. This expansion of horizons is attributed to the presence and power of the Holy Spirit.[38] In John's gospel, there are many would-be disciples, but the intimacy of the "beloved disciple" is the archetype of true discipleship.[39]

The prominence given to the theme of discipleship, with the world "disciple" used over 250 times in the four gospels and the Acts of the Apostles, now seems to disappear from the rest of the New Testament writings. Actually, discipleship has only just begun! For the message is that without baptism—expressive of the believer's death in the death of Christ and being risen in the risen Christ—the life of Christ cannot be shared without His indwelling Spirit. As Jesus gave back His Spirit to the Father in His death on the cross, so His followers have now received His Spirit at Pentecost, in their baptismal death. Then the epistles that follow teach the early church to express in differing ways the same process of becoming disciples, in dying and rising in Christ.

A Diverse Call to Christ

Paul speaks to the Corinthians of "imitating me as I imitate Christ." The Philippians likewise are to be "imitators of Christ." Becoming godly through Christ is the message to the Romans, walking with God is the theme to the Thessalonians, while the Colossians are assured, "Christ in you is the hope of glory." Kierkegaard was impressed, as we have seen, by the strongly ethical shape discipleship is given in the epistle of James, while Peter encouraged believers to accept the exile and journeying in faith that is entailed. Perseverance is the theme to the Hebrews, while the book of Revelation unites the theme of "the Way of the Lord" (or *Halakah*) throughout the Old Testament with "walking in the way of the Lamb."[40] In unison, all express a new humanity that is not self-contained nor self-grounded, but is a life "in Christ."

The call into the life of the risen Christ has always been diverse. But in the history of the church a curious interpretation arose when it was assumed it should be primarily the call into the monastic life. The life of Anthony (ca. 251–356) has been the prototype of this, when as a young man he responded to the call of the rich young ruler: "If you want to be perfect, go, sell your possessions and give to the poor.... Then come, follow me."[41] It became assumed that the life of "the religious" or those in religious vows lived "the more perfect form" of Christianity. There are many uncertainties for the future of the religious life, not least whether it is biblical in its textual assumptions, whether its traditions can face the future changes of society, and whether there can ever be held as valid this dualism of less and more perfect expressions of Christianity.[42] At the same time, how profoundly impoverished the church would have been without the depth and stability of devotion that the Christian monastic life has given to the world.

STAGES IN CHRISTIAN PERSONAL GROWTH

However, it is not in being different from others that a Christian is a Christian, but in being more fully alive, more truly human, because of Christ's love and His indwelling Spirit. For as the power of divine love moves differently from the power of the mind, so it is only by living within the presence of Christ that we can grow to become more truly persons than we were before. Christian "perfection" is not the Greek ideal of what is flawless; rather it is expressive of growth and maturity. For sanctity is simply the growth in baptismal grace, and the *sequela Christi,* or following Christ, is for everyone.[43]

Because He Loved First

It begins with divine attestation that we experience personally in conversion the reality: "He loved me and gave Himself for me!" Then in prayer and other expressions of devotion, we cultivate the presence of Christ. As we have already seen how vital unique recognition is to avoid narcissism, it is the recognition given us by Christ—as He gave to the woman who touched Him in the crowd or to Zacchaeus hiding in the tree—that is transforming indeed!

Further growth occurs with increasing self-understanding. Humility is the general environment for such emotional intelligence, that is, knowing oneself, one can read the hearts of others, too. Then one is more prepared to live within one's limits and self-acceptance, saying like the apostle, "By the grace of God I am what I am."[44] Again it is the mentoring friend who can help me to expose elements of self-deception and who can probe perhaps more deeply than I would wish to do voluntarily.

Good Listening

The role of listening remains critically important, as all good mentors know, for if language is so centrally expressive of our humanness, listening is its corollary. Yet good listeners are rare, for it is a humble and selfless role, too costly for most people. To listen truly requires relational skills to differentiate levels of communication: fact-centered complaints, projection, transference, obsessions, self-pity, and much more.[45] It implies we give an understanding context to the other. It is to enter actually the world of the other, which may require much patience, empathy, congruence, and even courage, as well as truthfulness and wisdom. The purpose of listening is more than healing, for it is also to enjoy a measure of self-transcendence. The exercise of kindness, in giving "space for the other to be" and in the desire to free the hearts of others, is a sign we are moving forward into the realm of beneficence, where love is being radiated selflessly.

Conformity to Christ, then, is the redemptive transformation of individuals becoming persons in a readiness to change. This begins in genuine response to the truth of God's Word, in contrition and docility. This deepens self-knowledge—not in the sterility of clinical self-examination, but in the fruitfulness and comfort of being confronted by God. True consciousness begins to transform us—not as with the antimodels we have examined, but as a response to the truth that is in Christ Jesus. True simplicity then begins to form, that is, the sense of inward unity, of single-hearted devotion to God, where He alone has primacy in thought and aspiration.[46] Humility then becomes our way of life, a humility that delights in the excellence of God that Jonathan Edwards has already shown us. The response deepens in love, both to God and to the neighbor, meaning that everyone is one's neighbor to be loved. This, observes Kierkegaard, is self-renouncing love, which is Christianity's essential form. It is also equality in loving, keeping no distinctions, as all being loved of God.[47] Christ made this His last prayer for us: "That they may be one as we are one.... That the love you have for me may be in them and that I myself may be in them."[48]

LETTER WRITING AS THE ART OF
NURTURING CHRISTIAN PERSONS

Only conformity to Christ makes selfless life truly possible as an "ecstatic life." One significant expression of this is Christian letter writing, which has been one of the longest traditions of mentoring in the history of Christianity.

Our Letters, Ourselves

John Donne (1572–1631) actually describes it as "a form of ecstasy," for it is of moving out of oneself to enter into the world of the other person. At the same time, he also suggests that "our letters are ourselves."[49] For we give of ourselves, as we give to the other, in our letters. The apostles, especially Paul, were concerned with the life situations of the Christian believers, as we read in so much of the corpus of the New Testament, a lasting model for all of us to "watch over yourselves and all the flock [of God]."[50]

In contrast to Derrida's skepticism about enduring friendship, Adam of Perseigne (d. 1221) writes to William, Bishop of Ely: "In the midst of (moral) catastrophe, ... to possess a friend is to have lost him" (i.e., if he, too, loses his Christian character, for then he can no longer be respected). Thus he encourages him to take a moral stand in the surrounding chaos: "So we are praying unceasingly for you."[51] Indeed, Adam esteemed spiritual friendship greatly, as he writes to a fellow abbot: "Love it is that is the entire topic between us, but it concerns that love for which virtue is the foundation, truth its study, purity its desire, piety its work, instruction in discipline its way of life," adding that while "love" "has more the sound of a natural faculty, 'charity' expresses the influence of grace."[52]

Augustine sets this focus clearly when he writes to Januarius:

> Use knowledge as a kind of scaffold by which to erect the building of love, which remains forever, even while knowledge is torn down. Knowledge, as a means to love, is highly useful: in itself, not as a means to such end, it has proven not only unnecessary but even harmful. I know, however, how your holy meditation keeps you safe under the shadow of the wings of the Lord our God.[53]

Yet Christian love is "tough love," as Fénelon writes to King Louis XIV:

> You can be a real follower of Christ only if you take the way of humiliation. You do not love God and your fear of him is base. You fear hell not God. Your religion is sheer superstition and pointless trivialities ... You love only your own glory and your own convenience. You think only of yourself, as if you were God and everything had been created to be sacrificed to please you. But God has created you only for the good of your own people. Unfortunately, you are blind to these truths. How can you see them when you do not know God, do not love him, do not pray to him from your own heart, and make no attempt to know him better?

In closing, Fénelon then says, "The man who writes these truths, Sire, scarcely wishes you misfortunes but instead would give his life to see you in a state that only God wishes you to be in. He will never cease praying for you."[54] More cryptically, the poet Gerard M. Hopkins once wrote to a worldly cleric, "Until you prefer God to the world and yourself you have not made the first step."[55]

However, even if we have learned some of the lessons against worldliness that Fénelon gave us so poignantly earlier in this book, we still need a change of mind-set. How hard it has been for the church not to remain influenced by Stoicism. Jerome, (347–420) writing to Eustochium (ca. 384), confesses:

> When I left home, parents, sister and relations for God's sake, I also left the comfortable style of life I was used to, to be a soldier of Christ. But I just couldn't do without a library that I had got together in Rome with so much effort ... I used to fast and read Cicero ... after countless tears for my past sins, I would reach for a nice volume of Plotinus. But when I reverted to my devotional style and took up one of the prophets to read, I couldn't bear the ghastly style!

(Augustine makes a similar confession as a youth.) Then Jerome was taken very seriously ill and he dreamed he was dead, facing the judgment day. The angelic host asked him,

> What are you?, so of course I replied, "a Christian!" The one on the judgment seat retorted: "Rubbish! You're no Christian—you're a Ciceronian! Where your treasure is, there your heart is also." What could I say?[56]

But Dietrich Bonhoeffer (d. 1945), facing his own death in a concentration camp, could see more clearly. Writing to a young friend shortly before he died, he said:

During these years the Church has fought for self-preservation as though it were an end in itself, and has thereby lost its chance to speak a word of reconciliation to humanity and the world at large. So our traditional language must perforce become powerless and remain silent, and our Christianity will be confined to praying and doing right to our human brothers and sisters. Christian thinking, speaking and organization must be reborn out of this praying and this action ... It will be a new language ... the language of a new righteousness and truth, which proclaims the peace of God with humankind and the advent of his kingdom.[57]

Blaise Pascal (1623–1662), writing to a lady, expands on this theme further:

A new language usually introduces a new heart. In his Gospel Jesus gave us a sign by which to recognize those who have faith. They will speak a new language. What happens is that a renewal of thoughts and desires brings about a renewal of language. Renewal is a constant necessity ... The old man in us dies away, says St. Paul, and is renewed each day, and will only be perfectly new in eternity ... It is certain that the graces God grants in this life are a sign of the glory which he prepares for us in the next.[58]

Humility, we have seen, is a vital expression of Christian devotion. Bernard of Clairvaux wrote a powerful treatise on "The Steps of Humility and Pride." But he wrote letters also about it. To a scholarly canon, he penned:

If you want the virtue of humility you must not
shun humiliations. If you will not suffer yourself
to be humbled, you can never achieve humility ...
Only the truly humble man can be said to restrain
himself, sparing his own soul, because he prefers
to conceal what he is, so that no one should
believe him to be what he is not. It is very dangerous for anyone to hear himself spoken of above
what he knows he deserves.[59]

Again, to the Patriarch of Jerusalem he wrote:

Only the humble man can safely climb the moun-
tain, because only the humble man has nothing to
trip him up. The proud man may climb it indeed,
yet he cannot stand for long ... to stand firmly, we
must stand humbly. So that our feet may never
stumble, we must stand, not on the single foot of
pride, but on the two feet of humility. Humility
has two feet: appreciation of divine power and
consciousness of personal weakness.[60]

Few have excelled the realism of Luther as he portrays
the Christian life, because for him God was real, and faith
was life lived under God. Sickness, bereavement, and
despondency were the order of the day, combined with the
persistence of depression he suffered personally. To a school-
master's wife he has invited to stay in his home, he writes:

You must not be so fearful and downhearted.
Remember that Christ is near and bears your ills,
for he has not forsaken you, as your flesh and
blood make you imagine. Only call upon him
earnestly and sincerely and you will be certain that
he hears you, for you know that it is his way to

> help, strengthen, and comfort all who ask him.
> Remember he has suffered far more for you than
> you can ever suffer for his sake or your own.[61]

In our own times, the letters of C. S. Lewis (1898–1963) are full of common sense and wit. To a lady he writes:

> I would prefer to combat the "I'm special" feeling
> not by the thought "I'm no more special than any-
> one else," but by the feeling "Everyone is as special
> as me." In one way there is no difference, I grant,
> for both remove the speciality. But the second
> leads to the truth that there isn't any crowd. No
> one is like anyone else. All are "members" (organs)
> in the Body of Christ. All different and all neces-
> sary to the whole and to one another: each loved
> by God individually, as if it were the only creature
> in existence. Otherwise you might get the idea
> that God is like the government which can only
> deal with the people in the mass.[62]

To another lady he responds: "You needn't worry about not feeling brave. Our Lord didn't—see the scene in Gethsemane. How thankful I am that when God became Man He did not choose to become a man of iron nerves: that would not help weaklings like you and me nearly so much."[63]

The emotions of the interior life have been the focus of much counsel, explored sweetly by Francis de Sales (1567–1622), submissively by Jean Pierre de Caussade (1675–1752), honestly by Gerhard Teersteegen (1697–1769). But the Abbé de Tourville (1842–1903) is confident of the presence and transcendence of God and also that self-giving is the essence of spiritual life. "The best thing is not to see your Lord do away with our difficulties," he writes, "as to see Him sustain us through them ... do not be distressed by lack of fervor and consolations. These will come in their own time and their own way." Indeed, we can let the good Abbé sum up the issues of this chapter quite simply:

> Our Lord wants you to become mature, and maturity needs these periods of obscurity, of disillusionment and boredom. Maturity comes when we have at last realized that we must love our Lord simply and freely in spite of our horrible unworthiness and of the unworthiness of nearly everything around us. Then a new and lasting Incarnation of our Lord takes place in our souls as it were. He begins to live a new life within us in the very midst of the misery of the world. That is why the greatest saints have always shown the perfect combination of nearness to our Lord on the one hand, and a deep sense of their own unworthiness and weakness on the other.[64]

Paganism required: Know yourself. Christianity declares: No, that is provisional—know yourself—and look at yourself in the mirror of the Word in order to know yourself properly. No true self-knowledge without God-knowledge or [without standing] before God.

—Søren Kierkegaard[1]

Scripture should so affect you, so pierce your heart, so work its way into your marrow, that it manifests that there is the true divine.

—John Calvin[2]

DISCIPLED BY THE WORD OF GOD

Kierkegaard has shown us how intrinsically relational we are, within as well as without ourselves. Self-consciousness is then a basic criterion for personal identity. But he argues that the state of despair, which is our sinful condition, is closely intertwined with self-consciousness, although it may take differing forms, according to our life-world, level of consciousness, or sexuality. At the Aesthetic level of living, the despair occurs when one is not conscious of being a self, in spite of all the vanity, conceit, and self-indulgence that are inherent in the Ulyssean lifestyle. In the moral or Stoic way of living, one is very willing to be oneself, even in defiance of God, as an autonomous agent. Here despair lies in the act of self-reconstructing, as late-modern therapy is now doing. The third level of consciousness is reflective mostly of the "spiritual" or "religious" ways multitudes live in the crowd, who despair in not being willing to be themselves, whether as males or females. This is reflective of their functional identities in "busyness," in programmatic lives, in fantasies of being "useful," self-important, or nurturing, and in other tricks of self-deception.

The "cure" or the resolution for Kierkegaard is theologically clear: "The self is healthy and free from despair only when, precisely by having despaired, it rests transparently in God."[3] But because despair is like no ordinary disease—for sin is its reality—it can be faced only by what the early Fathers called "the double Knowledge": knowing God and also knowing ourselves. It is well expressed in Augustine's prayer: "Let me know thee, O God, let me know myself, that is all!" It has been a central theme of the believing church, from the teachings of Clement of Alexandria through Origen, Ambrose, Augustine, Gregory the Great, Bernard of Clairvaux,[4] the late medieval mystics (notably Teresa of Avila), to John Calvin. Significantly, the seventeenth-century culture of neo-Stoicism challenged and ignored it, until Kierkegaard would remind us once more (as in our opening quotation), that there is "no true self-knowledge without God-knowledge."

MENTORED TO READ PERSONALLY

The essential ethical task, in the Socratic view, is coming to "know oneself." For the Gnostics later, it is to recognize the divine within oneself.[5] In contrast, Kierkegaard, faithful to the teachings of the Christian Fathers, emphasized that it is only by looking into "the mirror of God's Word" that "knowing oneself" is possible. Yet none of us can be innocent readers of God's Word. At the aesthetic level, we may use the Bible merely to reinforce our own immediate environment and self-regard. At the ethical level, we may use it like a "classic," ennobling our own moral and virtuous exploits. Or religiously, like the rabbinical tradition, we may view it as multiple levels, in the process of continual interpretation, such as psychoanalysis operates in therapy. All these avoid the actual personalizing of the text.

Quoting the ethical injunction of James 1:22–27, which says that we are to be "doers of the word, and not hearers only" (v. 22 KJV), Kierkegaard suggests that as readers we follow three steps to respond personally to the Bible.[6]

First of all, it is not just looking at the mirror, but also seeing ourselves in the mirror, and thus being challenged by what we see of ourselves being presented to us. The second step is that in everything we read, we should say continually, "It is I to whom it is speaking, it is I about whom it is speaking."[7] As Kierkegaard says, "The person who is not alone with God's Word is not reading God's word."[8] The third step, then, must be that "if you want to look at yourself in the mirror with true blessing, you must not forget how you looked, you must not be the forgetful hearer or reader."[9] Because it is God Himself who speaks, we are to obey His Word, to see and to know both ourselves and God, so that we can begin to live God-determined and indeed, God-shaped, lives. Then our Bible reading will relate to the "personal" rather than the Aesthetic, Ethical, or Religious life forms he has described for us so deeply.

A central biblical injunction will be familiar: "You shall not make for yourself an idol.... You shall not bow down to them or worship them" (Ex. 20:4–5). When we look into the mirror, to use Kierkegaard's parable, we do so either idolatrously or iconically. The Aesthetic, Moral, and Religious models he has described are all idolatrous, for they are all ways in which we see only ourselves—our own beliefs, our own values, our self-preoccupied lives. We can read the text of Scripture that way also, to bolster us in how we feel, think, and behave. We even call it "bibliolatry," for it is a form of idolatry. The mirror—the Bible—used in this way is an idol; it is man-made. It is dumb, dead, with a graven—not living—message.

The icon, however, is not a self-projection, but a revelation. It brings us a message from beyond, so we interpret and look at it differently. As Jean-Luc Marion has observed, the icon lets the visible image be "saturated" by the invisible, pointing us beyond itself.[10] The Greek words in the scriptural references to idol and icon demonstrate the contrast. *Eidolon* refers to "what is seen," known indeed by the fact that one has seen it, *oida*, an idol. But every icon (*eikon*) takes its norm from what the apostle Paul applies to Christ, the *eikon* of the invisible God (see Colossians 1:15). Although God remains invisible, His divinity shines through everything Christ said and did. Likewise, the text of Scripture is iconic; it is a witness to transcendence from transcendence. Kevin Vanhoozer sums it up neatly when he says, "To claim that the Bible is a verbal icon thus leads not to bibliolatry, but to the idea of Holy Scripture and to the idea that the text points away from itself."[11]

Marion likens the text of Scripture to a face, which resists attempts to master it, as one would try to "master" some theoretical knowledge. A face is to be "recognized" instead, and this is done by knowing someone personally. So could it be that the goal of reading the Bible is to have our lives drawn and directed to recognizing the face of Christ, whom we are learning to know personally? What matters is that the sense of the personal presence of Christ is made manifest in reading the text. Remember how Jesus Himself explained to the two disciples on the Emmaus road the presence of Christ in all the Scriptures. For they show us a face "that gazes at our gazes in order to summon them to its depth."[12] Moreover, the Scriptures not only point to Christ, but Christ is the only "true reader" of the Word. As Kierkegaard put it: "The Holy Scriptures are the highway signs: Christ is the way."[13]

READING BY THE RULE OF FAITH

When we look into Scripture as we look into a face, not merely looking at it, we see, says Kierkegaard, that it is indeed a "love letter." He insists that only when read as a word of love, with all its life-giving personal qualities that distinguish human beings—made in the image of God—can we be alone with the text and confronted by it. This is the approach that Irenaeus (140–200) first called "The Rule of Faith" for reading the Bible with understanding and obedience. By this he meant that we must interpret the Bible as one story, God's love story, and as having one central agent, the triune God of grace.[14] Thus Scripture must be interpreted accordingly, in the context of Father, Son, and Holy Spirit.[15] At first, the Israelites assumed it was their love story, "The Way of Israel." But once Christ is seen in all the Scriptures, as Luther saw the Bible afresh, then only the presence of the Holy Spirit, in the light of life, death, and resurrection of Jesus Christ, can generate such a profound change of consciousness.

Biblical thinking is thus contrasted to the deconstructive thinking that postmodernity now advocates. For us to determine what "makes sense" of the text is readily to see what we want to see and so to view it idolatrously. This excludes the biblical reader's response to its iconic character, which points us beyond our own ideology. As Stephen Moore has aptly put it, "Today, it is not our biblical texts that need demythologizing so much as our ways of reading them."[16] Rather the Rule of Faith consists of "listening to the God who speaks."[17] This commands communicative action, as we are exhorted not only to hear the Word but be doers of it. Reading the Bible is for the pursuit of godliness, not just to gain more information to reinforce our own life-world nor to remain within our own idolatrous status quo. So we distinguish it by calling it "theological reading," or *kerygmatic* reading within the profession of faith, as expressed by the biblical writers. For it comes as a royal proclamation, responded to by loyal subjects. Too many biblical scholars in Kierkegaard's age as well as today have tried to "explain" the Bible instead of "listening" to it in obedience. Kierkegaard would argue that such scholasticism has actually the effect of silencing the command of God's Word.

The grammar of biblical reading—that is, living by the Rule of Faith—interprets all things in the light of God's love. Human personhood is itself the gift of God's love and enables us to be communicants of that love. So individuals living "in sin," that is, living autonomously and faithlessly, cannot be "persons-of-the-Word," or "Torah persons," such as Psalm 119 depicts. For the "faithful" reader is one who needs basic trust in God in order to "delight" in God's Word "day and night." To be this kind of "reader," Kierkegaard gives us several points of advice.

- First, be "alone with God's Word," that is to say don't allow commentaries to get in the way of the text itself.
- Second, create silence for God's Word. Otherwise we forget it is God's Word, or else we cannot hear it above the "noises" of our own cultural dispositions.
- Third, regard it as the mirror in which we see and respond to what we see of ourselves as sinners.
- Fourth, this should lead us to a profound sense of conviction and lead us in personal repentance to read it

contritely, humbly open to God's message to us, and so to appropriate it personally.

- Fifth, read it responsively, to act upon it and "do the truth."
- Sixth, recognize the indirection of the biblical communication, as Jesus Himself spoke in parables. For thus the biblical narrative will draw us into its story-telling to participate within it and appropriate the message for ourselves.[18] For the truth cannot be imposed; it can only be appropriated personally.
- Finally, read it hopefully, believing "all things" are possible for God, so we are "open" to the "newness" of God.

This, then, is how Kierkegaard would have us "open" and "read" our Bible, to be discipled existentially by it. For discipleship itself is existential. It is not just informational in its posture and its intent. Christ Himself is "the true reader" of the Scriptures whose example we follow.

The Bible is thus God's story, having one central agent, the triune God.[19] Scripture must be interpreted accordingly, in the context of Father, Son, and Holy Spirit.[20] John Owen thus exhorted, "Let reading follow prayer." For if the purpose of Scripture is "to make us wise unto salvation," then its communicative action is to lead us to Christ, to abide in Him. As John Darr has pointed out, Theophilus (to whom Luke addressed his gospel and the Acts of the Apostles) is the ideal reader of Luke and Acts, for as "the friend of God," his very name is disposed to receive, witness to, and live out the message he has received. Reading the gospel becomes then a character-shaping reality.[21] But for the early church, the Scriptures were interpreted as the interaction of the past revelation (the Word) with the present revelation (the Holy Spirit), so that it was not the original text itself, but the text in the light of the advent of Jesus Christ.[22]

An icon, as we have seen, implies a reality beyond us, what George Steiner has called "presence" for "a Logos-order entails a central supposition of 'real presence.'"[23] So he has suggested that God somehow "underwrites" language to clarify its purpose from a divine point of view. Indeed, God's very being is a self-communicative act that enacts the covenant of discourse. For if God has spoken creation into existence by His Word, then all words can communicate substantially. Likewise, speech is the vital and unique personal gift of being human. Thus the first use of speech in early childhood is a great awakening. Rapidly it gives configuration of meaning to both our external and internal worlds, so we can begin to share, and by which we can accumulate knowledge cooperatively and be nurtured in our sociality.

But all our words are preceded by God's "speech." As Paul Beauchamp has put it:

> God did not so much create the things I am talking about, as He spoke them before speaking to me about them, so that the first human word might be declared to be a response to His ... By having God speak first, Genesis conceives of all human language as a response. A human being understands through his existence that he is God's image. And it is in his own speech that he declares that God has spoken. Giving the first word to God is the same as saying that the truth of human speech, on which it depends, cannot have any other depository than God Himself. Even human experience of language grasps it as repetition: no one would speak if those who gave him birth did not speak first.[24]

When God is denied His primal authority, knowledge is sought for in unusual places. Witness history's hermetic and Gnostic speculators, and Freud's search through dreams. Susan Handelman has called this "rabbinical displacement," for it substitutes one reality—God—for another, whether it be the "Torah" or some connectedness within the universe itself. It has contempt for plain meaning, preferring psychoanalytical meanings instead.[25] Rather, Jacques Ellul reflects, human speech has an eternal referent, "which it cannot escape from, without destroying itself or without stripping itself of all meaning. The value of the human word depends on the Word of God, from which it receives its decisive and ultimate character."[26] That is why the doctrine of *creatio per verbum,* creation by the Word, is of central importance to the mystery of creation.[27]

CANON AS SCRIPTURE WITHIN SCRIPTURE

Yet language gives shape to our view of God and of our world. It has flexibility, even indeterminate, so that the community of faith can accept, respond to, and incorporate the Word of God into their daily lives. The "canon of Scripture" (*kanon* in Greek means "measuring rod") refers to a list of authoritative or recommended books. They enclose, as it were, a space within which texts deemed authoritative can interact and inform one another. Its intertextuality reinforces and is consistent with what has gone before. Yet it also challenges old interpretations with potentially new or reformed meanings. It is thus expressive of the diverse ways this dialogue between God and humans has unfolded—communally so.

It is a "progressive revelation," not because God Himself is "in process," as some have speculated, but because human beings are in process—obediently, rebelliously, wisely, or foolishly so. God then has to "accommodate"

Himself, to speak "through the prophets at many times and in various ways."[28] Recent scholarship, led by Brevard Childs, has explored this contingent approach to Scripture.[29] The Bible's "holy" nature, as spoken of in the New Testament—making us "wise unto salvation"—is its "scriptural" character. Here Kierkegaard would remind us: "God's Word is given in order that you shall act in accordance with it, not in order that you shall practice the art of interpreting obscure passages!"[30] This is implied in the original meaning of the name *torah*, whose root meaning refers to *teaching*, that is, *actively instructing* in the most comprehensive way. It is not then merely about a "belief system," as Kierkegaard has been so strongly mentoring us to reject, but about living biblically.

The Pentateuch contains several codes, such as the Holiness Code of Moses (Leviticus 17—26) and the Great Code of the Law (Deuteronomy 12—26), especially the Ten Commandments, as well as earlier tribal codes. But these are embodied in the lives of the patriarchs and of God's covenant people as a way of life, *halakah*, a life-path, a way-of-being-in-the-world.[31] It is the Way of Life with the Creator-Redeemer. Living within Creation, where all things express the Word of God, the Pentateuch expresses this logocentricity in contrast to the naturalism of the surrounding paganism. It is a life, then, of "keeping the commandments of the Lord thy God" and of "walking with God." This is first illustrated in the lives of Enoch, Noah, Abraham, and then Moses, as well as in later expressions of the covenant life of Israel as a whole.[32]

THREEFOLD FORMS OF OLD TESTAMENT INSTRUCTION

Later, toward the end of the progress of canonization, we are given an interesting hint in Jeremiah 18:18 of this development of Scripture, as reflecting upon three distinct types of believing communities.

> The Torah shall not perish from the priest,
>> "nor counsel from the wise,
>> nor the word from the prophets."

These refer to three shapes of biblical knowledge that are expressive of the whole educational process of Israel, whose principles we can readily apply in biblical mentoring today.

First, the Torah has the basic authority of being catechetical and foundational in the formation of the covenant people of God. It is the disclosure of what is binding upon the family, like Israel, in daily remembrance.[33] The Shema, an ancient prayer, is also this "shorter catechism" for Israelite children to learn from infancy, by recitation and embodiment: "Hear, O Israel: The LORD our God, the LORD is one. Love the LORD your God with all your heart and with all your soul and with all your strength."[34]

As an act of reflection, the memory of Israel is deepened, not only in such inner reflection of prayer in the Shema, but also in encountering historical events, with reminders of the past stories of the patriarchs, the exodus, and their own narrators. So we walk through Genesis alongside Enoch, Noah, and Abraham, "who walked with God." Exodus speaks of the renunciation of the pagan ways of Egypt as liberation indeed! Leviticus celebrates the basic necessity of sacrifice in cultic life. Numbers is a dynamic book, early given the title "In the Wilderness," for it speaks to the need of fortitude and perseverance, while the Promised Land lies still ahead. Deuteronomy is retrospective education that helps us keep on "remembering." For "as a parent disciplines a child so the LORD your

God disciplines you. Therefore keep the commandments of the LORD your God, by walking in his ways and by fearing him."[35] The "fear of the Lord" is cultic, moral, and legal fear, the "grammar" of covenant attitudes that are foundational for the obedient before God. It is a "fear" to preserve us from sin, to give us a "heart for God alone," in humility and loyal commitment, indeed to be the foundation for a relationship with God.[36] It conveys all that is meant by "godliness."

Torah education is very sure and assertive, for it is grounded in the law of the Lord. It provides the ground for solidarity and community life before God. Questions of identity, such as plague us today, are foreign to those who truly are "Torah persons." However, we realize that fixture of certitude and rigidity of traditional attitudes can deteriorate such education into the commonplace and the nominal, as the unexamined religious life.

This is why we constantly need a second biblical element, that is, prophetic voices to protest against royal rationality in Israel, or against denominational bureaucracy today, or against the substitution of the living Word for scholarly compendia "about doctrine," for they are all self-serving.

Thus this new, second sense of the Word of the Lord is required, which appears between the eighth and fifth centuries BC. It is voiced by courageous, selfless persons like Amos, Micah, Jeremiah, Ezekiel, and Daniel, among many others. Because their testimony is tested by their lives to be truly inspired, their writings are later canonized. Seventeen of the thirty-nine books of the Old Testament are thus incorporated as the canon of the conscience of Israel. For the true prophets realize that sin is definable only in the context of a personal God, Yahweh, and that the worst forms of sin can actually be within the context of worship. "Go to Bethel and sin; go to Gilgal and sin yet more," challenges Amos.[37] Instead of "thousands of rams" and "ten thousand rivers of oil," Micah simplifies it all as one of having right relationship: "To act justly and to love mercy and to walk humbly with your God."[38] Thus alone among the Old Testament Scriptures "and unique among the sacred texts of other religions," the Bible catalogs the iniquities of the very people whom the book calls "chosen," "holy," and "beloved" of God.[39]

Third, there is the group of books called the Writings (*kethubim*) that deals with other contingencies of covenant life. They appear a miscellaneous collection of materials, without the apparent coherence of the other books, named "the counsel of the wise." Wisdom is primarily exercised in liminal situations of life, that is to say, of life on the frontiers, facing unprecedented experiences, perhaps also in dangerous situations such as life at the court, with its treacherous relationships, or in facing intellectual problems unrealized before, or when tragedy strikes, all of which could readily lead to catastrophe. All are symbolic of the "chaos" that the Creator overcame by His Word. A heavily socialized conformity does not equip us to be "streetwise." For Job in his moral crisis, it is vital then to have an answer to "Where can wisdom be found?"[40] Learning at this level cannot be found in dogmatic responses such as those Job's friends too easily gave him.

ANTICIPATION OF A NEW ERA

This is the time to attain new insights that can penetrate through perplexity, to gain deeper confidence through inscrutability, and to listen to the narratives of others with more discernment. So we can learn to compare the lives of Saul and of David in order to shape our own moral attitudes wisely. Reading the life of Samuel, we are struck by the centrality of prayer as the key element from his birth to all his ministry and guidance of Israel. Yet all these insights and more are gained only through humility and obedience in order to see life from a divine perspective. Therefore the limits of human capacity, the futility of self-interest, the complexity of human emotions, must all be identified "in the presence of the Lord," as the psalmist illustrates to us. It is all summed up in the basic reflection of the psalmist:

> But as for me, I trust in You, O LORD,
> I say, "You are my God."
> My times are in Your hand.[41]

Yet "the wisdom of the wise" was not enough for the leaders of Israel to understand and accept Jesus Christ within their "way of Life." Now the biblical canon is given its greatest challenge, in the most radical reinterpretation. Humanly speaking, it seemed unimaginable, yet also most desired!

JESUS CHRIST IN ALL THE SCRIPTURES

The New Testament claims that Christ is the Word of God. It begins with Jesus' own claim when He started His ministry in His hometown of Nazareth. Reading from the prophet Isaiah He proclaims: "The Spirit of the Lord is on me, because he has anointed me to preach good news to the poor." He concludes with the stunning words: "Today this Scripture is fulfilled in your hearing."[42] The dawning recognition of His messianic claims fills the narratives of the Gospels.

The man who wrote no book is yet "the Man of the

Book," who has radically reinterpreted the symbols, aspirations, promises, and life of His people. Ever since, "Christ crucified" has been "a stumbling block to Jews and foolishness to Gentiles."[43] Now all the stages and genres of the canon, as Prophet, Priest, and King, as the Word of God, and as the Wisdom of God, indeed all of Scripture, these are now personified in Jesus Christ.[44]

Much can be gained in studying the life and ministry of Jesus within the praxis of His person as a prophet.[45] The Bible also gains so much depth when we see it through the conflicts that Jesus faced and was challenged by in first-century Judaism.[46] Only in such depth can we appreciate more clearly Jesus' own words to His hearers: "Do not think that I have come to abolish the Law or the Prophets; I have not come to abolish them but to fulfill them."[47]

The Acts of the Apostles show us that it is only by the gift of the presence of the Holy Spirit that it was, and still is, possible to accept, to believe, and to spread this new hermeneutic with its revolutionized typology of "Christ the key to all the Scriptures," as He shows Himself to be on the road to Emmaus. Paul the apostle, by his conversion on the Damascus road, by his rabbinical training, by his human weakness, and yet by his gift of the Holy Spirit and acceptance within the believing community, can now focus upon this radical reinterpretation of the law, in the light of Christ.[48] He did this by focusing upon all the Old Testament symbols as being open and anticipatory. They all foreshadow Christ: the exodus, the wilderness, the Promised Land, the temple, the priesthood, the sacrifices—all the elements of Israelite identity, life, history, and worship.

Christ, by His Spirit, now communicates both typologically and personally in ways that become essential for the early fathers of the church to pass on. So it was by the use of such biblical allegory, skillfully preached by Ambrose, that Augustine confessed:

> Above all, I heard first one, then another, then many difficult passages in the Old Testament figuratively interpreted, where I, by taking them literally had found them to kill. So after several passages in the Old Testament had been expounded spiritually, I now found fault with that despair of mine, caused by my belief that the law and the prophets could not be defended at all against the mockery of hostile critics.[49]

Augustine is of course referring to Paul's statement, "The letter kills, but the Spirit gives life."[50] In monotheism, this is a dangerous statement, for it detracts from the authority of the text into what could be judged "private interpretation," a euphemism for "subjective emotionalism." Whose "spirit"? Whose imagination? But Jesus had promised His disciples that at His departure He would not leave them bereft, for He would send another "Comforter," a Mentor indeed, who would "lead them into all truth." Rabbi as Saul had been, now Paul the apostle, together with the early Christian community that received him into their fellowship—all were now recipients of the self-same Spirit, Spirit of God, Spirit of Christ, and indeed the Spirit of Wisdom. It was the Spirit alone who opened their hearts to receive the mind of God.[51]

The Spirit's Presence

It is this confession of faith in Christ that still makes the Spirit's advent possible in the lives of all believers. In turn, He makes the reality of Christ's abiding presence in the believers through His Word their own experience. The Spirit also binds all believers to Christ, as "one spirit" with Him.[52] It is with this triune authority alone that the revolutionary reinterpretation of the Scriptures first given by Jesus can now give the apostles boldness to write their epistles as also the Word of God. For their unique focus, intent, and purpose is only to proclaim the good news of Jesus Christ. As a result, no book before or since has claimed for itself Christ the Word of God, as also "Christ in all the Scriptures."

MENTORED BY THE CONTINGENCY OF THE SCRIPTURES

Confronting the Greek world directly, Paul brought the language and grammar of faith into the utterly contrasted realm of Hellenism, which had no personal logocentricity, no personal God, no Creator nor Savior. So Eric Auerbach makes a striking contrast between the Aesthetic level of Homer's *Odyssey* and the Old Testament personal level of narrative given of Abraham and Isaac on Mount Moriah:

> Far from seeking, like Homer, merely to make us forget our own reality for a few hours, it seeks to overcome our reality: we are to fit our own life into this world, feel ourselves to be elements in its structure of universal history ... Everything else that happens in the world can only be conceived as an element in this sequence, into it everything that is known about the world ... must be fitted as an ingredient of the divine plan.[53]

Everything in the Aesthetic consciousness of Homer takes place in the foreground, visible, palpable, with nothing hidden or unexpressed, in an absolutely temporal present. By contrast, in the biblical narrative everything is indeterminate and contingent: time and space, motives and purposes are unexpressed—in Auerbach's phrase "fraught with background" or in Steiner's phrase "full of presence."

Homer can only be analyzed, as psychoanalysis does, but it cannot be interpreted iconically, for it has no "canon." But in biblical narrative, there is a linear direction forward, so that the past is determined by the future, in what is termed an "eschatological orientation." Yet the Bible points inwardly also, to its own inner network of interconnectedness, so that what is required is to listen to the text not in vision or abstraction, but with one's own heart.

Being "in Christ"

As we have recognized, the logocentricity to the text is intrinsically contingent. "For all things were created by the Word of his power," not in capriciousness, but in love. So Paul could declare to the Greeks Him in whom "we live and move and have our being."[54] Yet that contingency itself is also the ground for believing that He knows what we need before we ever ask Him. Need we wonder, then, that "in Christ," as the apostle loved to identify the believers, our contingency will be perfected?

Writing to the Roman Christians, the apostle Paul expresses his great grief that his fellow countrymen had done the wrong kind of reading in not interpreting the Scriptures as God's love letter and therefore in not recognizing personally that divine righteousness lies within the law of God, not apart from it. "Brothers, my heart's desire and prayer to God for the Israelites is that they may be saved," Paul writes, for "Christ is the end of the law," that is, its fulfillment by entering into a right relationship with God.[55] Then he shows how contingent God's Word is to us:

> The righteousness that is by faith says: "Do not say
> in your heart, 'Who will ascend into heaven?'"
> (that is, to bring Christ down) "or 'Who will
> descend into the deep?'" (that is, to bring Christ
> up from the dead). But what does it say? "The
> word is near you; it is in your mouth and in your
> heart," that is, the word of faith we are proclaiming: That if you confess with your mouth, "Jesus is
> Lord," and believe in your heart that God raised
> him from the dead, you will be saved. For it is
> with your heart that you believe and are justified,
> and it is with your mouth that you confess and are
> saved. As the Scripture says, "Anyone who trusts in
> him will never be put to shame."[56]

Paul, the exegete, is using Deuteronomy 30:11–14, as well as Leviticus 18:5 to show that, far from the law having been set aside in place of Christ, it promises the same relatedness to God as Christians now have in Christ: belief in the heart is the crucial issue in the Old Testament as now in the New Testament. Then confession of the basic faith will follow as the outer manifestation of this critical inner response.[57] Yet the pathos for the apostle, as we may have also with loved ones who do not read Scripture as God's love letter to us, is that the very people to whom Moses proclaims the nearness of the Word, whose hearts God promises to circumcise (Deut. 30:6), are also a "perverse generation" (see Deut. 32:20). So near, and yet so far away!

No Room for Self-Autonomy

"You are near, O LORD, and all Your commandments are

truth"[58] is the conviction of the person discipled by the Word. Indeed, such is the contingency of God's Word in all aspects of life that the psalmist uses eight synonyms in Psalm 119 to express all the nuances and needs to express covenant relationship with God. As the apostle has already emphasized, the heart is the home of the real self in the Bible, the "I" that we sinfully interpret as the control center of our own being. But the psalmist's "Thou" refers to the One who should be our control center, not the "I." "Thou" represents also the contingency of God's presence, before whom we stand in whatever mood, feeling, emotion, passion, and circumstance we may be experiencing.

The directness of address, "I" to "Thou," then leaves no place for self-autonomy; rather it moves forward in obedience and trust to become "I" *in* "Thou." For this polemic against the isolated self, the narcissistic self, is also a shelter of abiding trust, strong comfort, and deepest understanding or empathy, so there develops a uniquely intimate relatedness between the soul and God.[59] It is the prayer of Hezekiah, who in his political helplessness can only acknowledge God: "You are the God, You alone.... You alone, O LORD, are God."[60]

Human Experience Mirrored

Shy and taciturn as John Calvin was as a person, he came to recognize the Psalms as the "Anatomy of all the parts of the Soul":

> Since there is no emotion anyone will experience
> Whose image is not reflected in this mirror.
> Indeed, here the Holy Spirit has drawn to life
> All the pains, sorrows, fears, doubts, hopes, cares, anxieties—
> In short—all the turbulent emotions with which men's minds are commonly stirred.[61]

Thus Calvin came to see how the psalmist disciples us profoundly in all the grammar of faith. For this grammar sets real limits in humility to our creatureliness. Yet it also "makes sense" at all levels of our person: mentally in remembering the ways of God in His historical actions; connatively—that is, in the exercise of the will—in guiding us to choose willingly between the senselessness of being either willful or of being will-less; and emotionally, in spite of despair, despondency, envy, anger, and many other negative feelings, moods, and passions that may come over us. So the grammar of faith is also a convincing word, as "a lamp to my feet and a light for my path."[62]

Yet the contingency of God's Word, as Ezekiel realizes, must be also radical enough to give us both a heart transplant—a "new heart"—as well as a "new spirit." The psalmist and the prophets so exposed themselves to God that they encourage, yes, drag us also "before the Lord," to "cleanse the heart," to "renew the heart," and to "strengthen the heart."

With all these enriching series of biblical insights, the apostle Paul is further aware of the advent of the Holy Spirit at Pentecost to the believing community and to himself. So "walking in the Spirit" has a new depth that still links him with the patriarchs, but now also with his own personal experience too. His ethical admonitions are couched in "the practice of the Spirit,"[63] as a comprehensive pattern of action governed by a Christian perspective on all of life. This is decisively "from above," originating in the Spirit and Word of God, objectively so, and yet it is also "from below," in the believer's responses, walking obediently and freely before the Lord. A life of prayer becomes then the full expression of such personal living.

Strength in Weakness

Evangelical contingency is also centrally expressed in the

theological motif of weakness (*astheneia*), which implies natural illness and powerlessness. But Paul uses it also spiritually in terms of creation with our dependence on our Creator, as well as in terms of redemption, for we are incapable of fulfilling the law. Yet weakness is the place where our lives can become theocentric, for it is where God meets us in our need and therefore where His grace and power are perfected.[64]

This, then, is no abstraction. Just as the apostle actually experienced this throughout his personal narrative, we too can fully enter into it—to experience the full realism of the good news of God's grace. Indeed, living "under the cross" of Christ's own weakness is the badge of the greatest apostolic authority for Paul, who had been tempted, perhaps often, to consider himself an "outsider," even "a freak of nature"![65]

No one can be more "inside the faith" than the one who also experiences most personal weaknesses and yet sees them most meaningfully addressed by the Word of God, in the grace of Christ, and by the power of the Holy Spirit. We give the last word to the apostle Paul:

> For power is brought to its end in weakness. All the more gladly will I glory rather in my weakness, in order that the power of Christ (instead of my own feeble power having ended) will take up residence/tabernacle in me.[66]

To worship is to quicken the conscience by holiness …
to feed the mind with all the truth of God … to purge the imagination
by the beauty of God … to open the heart to the love of God …
and to devote the will to the will and purpose of God.

—Archbishop William Temple

DISCIPLED FOR
WORSHIP IN
COMMUNITY

Our survey of the ways metaethical systems of the past have shaped our Western identity and "mentored" each of us is by no means the end of the story. For in our own day, the identity of the Christian has become more confused than ever—and is in flux. We have allowed such an admixture of motives and attitudes, of commitments and detachments, of sacrifices and ambitions, of spiritual and materialistic values, of personal and institutional perspectives, that all those who claim to believe the Apostles' Creed can differ so widely as to seem from different planets.

This is perhaps most critically tested by our differing interpretations of, and attitudes toward, worship. As Stephen Sykes has noted:

> The variety of roles which are presented to an indi-
> vidual, irrespective of whether that person could ever
> come to occupy them all, constitutes a severe threat
> to the single-mindedness required in the perform-
> ance of religious obligations. Religious observance
> increasingly resembles a rather inefficiently organized
> leisure-time activity, made available for those with a
> particular preference, and the practitioners of religion
> appear to accord it no higher priority than might be
> claimed by a tennis club.[1]

WORSHIP IN ITS APOCALYPTIC CONTEXT

Some of us prefer worship to be "high"—with "smells," "bells," and Gregorian chants. Some of us like it "low"—with our guitars and our casual songs. "Inspirational" may mean "entertainment"; "freedom of spirit" may imply our individualism; and "a good program" may represent strong, central control. What is true worship?

True worship is contingent upon the Creator, and it is also expressive of gratitude to the Lamb, our Redeemer Jesus Christ who lives eternally as truly man and truly God. What Jesus Christ has done historically, God does eternally (the one "who is, and who was, and who is to come"[2]). Thus the church does not exist for itself, but it is both illustrative of and instrumental to the eternal reign of God's kingdom. It is this that is truly climactic of the Christian's mentored life: to worship the triune God forever and ever.

In the book of Revelation, John writes at the end of the first century to "the seven churches," the local and the particularized churches we all reflect universally. Worship of the Lamb should express the communion of saints, said John the Seer.[3] Yet that is not all. He also writes that worship actually judges and separates human beings, for it reveals conflict of cosmic proportions.

He indicts our own aberrations and distortions of what "worship in spirit and in truth"[4] really should be. For Christ with His relentless revelation of "the way and the truth and the life" walks among us, observes our real condition (Rev. 2:2), and with His eyes of fire discerns our inner motives and attitudes (2:19). He reproves us for having a false reputation (3:1), for self-deception (3:17), for being slanderous of others (2:9), and of accommodating to the ways of the world.

Against all this, Richard Bauckhman observes:

> Revelation's prophetic critique is of the churches as much as of the world. It recognizes that there is a false religion not only in the blatant idolatries of power and prosperity, but also in the constant danger that true religion falsify itself in compromise with such idolatries and betrayal of the truth of God.[5]

The truth of God is known only in the worship of God alone, in and through His Spirit. True worship contrasts Creator and creature, transcendence and finitude, heavenly glory and earthly idols. But to gain this perspective, John—and his readers with him—has to be taken up into the heavens in order to appreciate worship from an apocalyptic perspective. The message is such that it requires apocalyptic terms—a genre to convey a transcendent reality revealed by an otherworldly Being.[6] For true worship is most radically theocentric, or else it is self-worship: sinful and the most anthropocentric and narcissistic expression of human rebellion against God.

Worship Determines Our Lives

If, then, the primary act of worship is the recognition of our Creator above all created idols, there is also its redemptive and saving purpose. The uniqueness of Christian worship lies in the incomparability of divine love, which we celebrate in the death of Christ. We recall, then, in prayer and praise, the accomplishment of divine grace. As recollection, it is based upon memory, whereas secularized "worship" is in quest of novelty, according to current, upbeat musical fashions, and with little or no sense of gratitude. In that setting it is not likely that we would be reminded of the prophetic indictment: "These people honor me with their lips, but their hearts are far from me."[7]

Christian worship inevitably must pay much attention to inwardness, to the issues of the "heart." As Charles Wesley would have us sing, "O for a heart to praise my God, a heart from sin set free." Such worship challenges intentions, exposes pride, seeks humility, expresses dependence, and deepens trust. It's the antithesis of many contemporary forms of worship, whose goal is to not "put us to sleep" with programs that are barely more than "showbiz." They lose sight of the real purpose of religious worship by celebrating human institutions instead.

Worship Is Communal

But there is another element in Christian worship: its communality. Worship is what befits all the people of God, who together acclaim "Our Father." Individualism has no place at the Lord's table. It is a characteristic our Lord condemned in the disciples at the Last Supper. Likewise, the apostle Paul chided the Corinthians for their so-called "love feasts," based on their carnal way of life. Their self-indulgent, self-centered, self-referential focus was in utter contrast to the self-giving love and humility of Christ Himself. Likewise, he rebuked the Galatians for being conceited, competitive, and envious of each other (see Gal. 5:26). Clearly, such situations inhibited any possible communality, not to mention eliminating gratitude to the Savior and Lord.

But this cancerous egotism—which the apostle calls "the flesh"[8]—is what marks our contemporary society. This should give us as much sense of foreboding, as John discerned this evil was tearing apart the Roman society in his day.

As our society becomes increasingly individualistic, fragmented, and pluralistic, the diversity of liturgies, the loss of common traditions, the increasing forms of experimentation, all put an increasing strain on the synchronic unity of Christian worship, that is, on worshipping at the same time, in a common unity of expression. How communal can Christian worship remain? Moreover, all four elements of worship—freedom, commitment, interiority, and communality—are threatened by such changes. It is well-known, observes Hans Mol, that competition between a large variety of foci of identity leads to a lack of spontaneity and commitment, a loss of identity, and a sense of meaninglessness, anomie, and alienation in which community disappears.[9]

To speak then of "communal worship" is more hopeless than even seeking community of belief. Perhaps that is why we are witnessing such pathetic efforts to seek to affirm it artificially by manipulative organization. Instead, all it does is shallow out any true sense of "personal identity," "worship," or "community." Perhaps a celibate priest or some self-sacrificial trait of the officiating worship leader can contribute to some semblance of unity of worship in the "sacrifice of praise," even when the covert opposition to spontaneity, commitment, self-examination, and living a shared life in Christ is strongly felt to be present.

Worship Is Universal and Cosmic

John the Seer takes community of worship much further yet. For it is not only expressive of the people of God which He has called unto Himself, but also of a universal gathering of all the nations. As the prophet Zechariah anticipates:

> "Shout and be glad, O Daughter of Zion. For I am coming, and I will live among you," declares the Lord. "Many nations will be joined with the Lord in that day and will become my people. I will live among you and you will know that the Lord Almighty has sent me to you."[10]

The cost of true worship has been martyrdom for many of God's people, but their "sacrifice of praise" will be vindicated by the conversion of the nations to the ways of the Lord. As a result of their faithful witness, even as Christ Himself is "the true and faithful witness," all peoples will become God's people. John expresses it this way:

> The glory of God gives it light, and the Lamb is its lamp. The nations will walk by its light, and the kings of the earth will bring their splendor into it. On no day will its gates ever be shut, for there will be no night there. The glory and honor of the nations will be brought into it.[11]

This is God's vision of true worship for mentored Christians and of its effects, present and future. How then are we discipled to become a "kingdom of priests," who are not merely "Aesthetic," nor "Stoic," nor just "Religious" in worship?

I have found three significant mentors to rebuke and redirect our "natural" worship. Two we've met before in this book: Jonathan Edwards and Bernard of Clairvaux. One is new: Hans Urs von Balthasar.

WORSHIP FROM THE HEART

As we saw in chapter 3, Jonathan Edwards was a child of the Enlightenment yet also free from its distortions of faith. Reaction to the religious wars of the seventeenth century—

like the militancy of religious fundamentalists today—spawned during that time a popular desire for deism. People sought a religion of reason—acceptable for "reasonable minds"—to demonstrate God's existence. This was a time, or so taught John Locke, when incipient democracy required individual freedom of thought to challenge the church's monopoly on truth. A quest for universals—which left open the practices and beliefs of other religions and which in its Unitarian character ignored the person of Christ—was also associated with a Pelagian spirit of moral self-improvement. We can see today how these ideas have resulted in intensified modern individualism.

Edwards, as we have seen, interpreted all this as the counterfeit of true religion, which had no "spiritual knowledge," no "sense of the heart," no personal awareness of God's abiding presence within oneself. Reason might seek to prove the existence of God, but it could not warm the heart. Nor could it see the singularity of God in His divine beauty, to engender "gracious affections" experienced in consistency with God's Word. Nor could this idolatrous worship recognize the Holy Spirit's special work within the believer to convert, to make holy, and to transform our consciousness, so that we love and appreciate God above and beyond all other.

As Edwards read Locke's theories of language and knowledge, he realized Locke could open only one room of human consciousness, that of cognition. Locke's followers can only carry "the notion of doctrine in their heads," so that "to be fluent, fervent, and abundant in words, in talking of the things of religion" may be just that, "the religion of the mouth and the tongue." Just talk![12]

Here Edwards is remarkably close to how Søren Kierkegaard has already mentored us, when the latter says true worship "does not consist in singing, and hymning, and composing verses."[13] Words and thoughts alone can never serve as means of divine grace, nor can language adequately express our true life before God. For as Pascal put it a century before Edwards: "The heart has its reasons that reason knows not of."

In the midst of a religious revival that proved ephemeral in the lives of too many "converts," Edwards wrote to mentor his congregation about the nature of true or "gracious" affections for God. He noted that their fervency of spirit and abundance of experiences could still be all false, not a true sense of the heart before God.[14] For to have "gracious affections" involves the sanctification of the will, to be "made holy" in the communication and personal possession of new, godly affections and desires, something that deists could never imagine. This implies the sanctification of the reasoning faculty to overcome egocentricity and its own prejudices and to be given new light to appreciate the beauty or singularity of God, in the presence of Christ, by the indwelling of the Holy Spirit.

Only the gift of the Holy Spirit can make the beauty and goodness of God so winsome and attractive to us that we in turn are given an inner symmetry of personal godliness to make us also "something beautiful for God." Moreover, the practical effect of the Holy Spirit in the life of the Christian results in a practiced faith. Only such personal holiness of living, not merely clarity of mind, is what will keep the Christian from falling into such error, as Kierkegaard depicted later in his three categories of false forms of consciousness.

WORSHIP IN SELFLESS LOVE

If self-love, as the morality of our sinful nature, fails to satisfy the human heart, then union with Christ alone makes one a whole person. But God-centeredness in its new sense of being implies that true virtue is to be one in God's love. No one has been more passionately aware of this than Bernard of Clairvaux, with whom we became familiar in chapter 6. For if Kierkegaard has opened us to our own inner relatedness, Augustine has explored how deeply God enters into our inner being, and Edwards has argued "the very quintessence of religion ... is LOVE," then Bernard mentors us in the "school of love."

If "God is love," as the apostle John has affirmed He is, then being created in the "image and likeness of God" implies for Bernard that it is love, more even than mere intelligence, that reflects the basis of God's intent to relate to us in friendship.

As Edwards does, Bernard first insists upon the primary importance and the value of personal experience of God. He eulogizes throughout his sermons in *On the Song of Songs,* as he teaches his novitiates: "Today, the text we are to study is the book of our own experience." Then he challenges us to describe what we have experienced of the intimacy of Christ's love.[15]

Although fifteen years his elder, William of St. Thierry was profoundly challenged by Bernard's remarkable spiritual insights.[16] One was about the return of Christ, which the early church anticipated as "soon." Thus Christ's lovers, like Bernard and medieval saints for the next four hundred years, might sigh with the Lover in the book of Song of Songs for the return of the Beloved. But Bernard reminds us of Christ's threefold advent: first in the flesh, then His epiphany in glory, but meanwhile His daily visits to us in His Word.[17] In Sermon 74, Bernard therefore argues:

> Show me a soul which the Bridegroom, the Word, is accustomed to visit often, whom friendship has made bold, who hungers for what has once been tasted, and without hesitation I will assign it to the voice and name of the Bride.[18]

Second, Bernard goes further, for if we experience God's love, we know it in a Trinitarian form. He interprets Matthew

11:27 as one of the most profound statements of the Scriptures: "No one knows the Son except the Father, and no one knows the Father except the Son." The arrogance of Bernard's contemporary Abelard and other scholars who would presume to explore the mystery of the Trinity merely by their own wits is duly exposed as pride. For, argues Bernard, "it is the Holy Spirit indeed, who is the love and benign goodness"[19] of the Father and the Son.

As in Augustine's writing, the desire for God is a third great theme in Bernard's teaching.[20] Both share four aspects of this: (1) It is absence that intensifies desire. (2) The experience of desire is affective, for it is located in the will more than in the intellect. (3) The desire for God originates from a basic human need, as an imperative of our creaturely being and not merely as a simple option of the will. And (4) the desire for God finds its ultimate consummation in the eternal state, so it is essentially eschatological in orientation.

As Bernard sums it up, "God himself is love, and nothing created can satisfy the human being who is made to the image of God, except the God who is love, who alone is above all created natures."[21]

Fourth, Bernard interprets divine love as providing the constitution and shape of the spiritual life of the Christian worshipper. As we have seen of the virtuous life of the Stoics, variable ethical values can be selected under the cultural pressures we live in. But love alone denotes the necessary progress toward godliness. If God is love, Bernard asks, then how can Love not be loved?

> Rightly then, she (the Christian) renounces all other affections and devotes herself to love alone, for it is in returning love that she has the power to respond to love. Although she may pour out her life in love, what is that compared to the inexhaustible fountain of God's love?[22]

All we can hope to do, then, is to progress by simple steps from one degree of perception to another, our progress being marked by deepening humility which expresses more and more our release from an ego-centered or proud identity toward an increasingly exocentric calling. This is what Paul would define our new identity to be "in Christ."

Four Stages of Spiritual Progress

Finally, in his treatise *On Loving God,* Bernard outlines four stages of spiritual progress toward selflessness. Alas it should be so, but human love begins by serving itself first. It is indeed "carnal love," what the apostle calls "life according to the flesh," described by Thomas Merton as being "rooted in our own psychic automatism." So even when we appreciate something of the love of God, it is what Bernard calls "loving God for our own sake." Bernard is prepared to treat this self-disposition kindly because of our human frailty. Even love of one's neighbor may be prudentially included in this first stage, as boosting each other up. Next comes the second stage, of loving God for our own sake as a matter of prudence of knowing what one can and cannot do by oneself. We see that only God can help us in some circumstances.

Then in the third stage, we become more aware of, and eventually influenced by, God's selfless love, so we begin to love Him for His own sake. Only then will the love of God make it possible to love our neighbor selflessly. As Bernard writes: "Tasting God's sweetness entices us more to pure love than does the urgency of our own needs."[23] We say, then, the experience of ongoing conversion helps us to begin "to love God for His own sake," truthfully and purely. No longer is it a necessitous love, so the freedom to enter into this third stage occurs with the growth of voluntary desire for God alone. Slowly we begin to abandon self-reliance, now being drawn, as Edwards has shown us, by the beauty of

God, or by what Bernard calls God's charm or *suavitas*. As Bernard puts it: "'Confess to the Lord, for He is good' (Psalm 117:1). Who confesses to the Lord, not because He is good to him but because the Lord is good, truly loves God for God's sake and not for his own benefit."[24] This climax comes only when selflessness grows from such preoccupation with God's love that one lives in unconscious self-forgetfulness, absorbed in the personal experience of God, in unceasing worship of the Lamb, and in longing only to be one in communion and union with God. Bernard believes that, in general, this is the highest stage of love Christians experience on earth.

The fourth stage, of "loving ourselves as God loves us," is a sheer gift of God's grace, not something that can ever come from our own efforts. The martyrs may have experienced it "partially," Bernard suggests. He admits he has also tasted of this experience. It is fully for the life to come of mystical and eternal union with God—and yet glimpsed at in the contemplative life—we can begin to experience God's love. Such a contemplative life helps us to love ourselves only for God's sake, which now also implies that we no longer treat ourselves neurotically as we have been sinfully treated. Now we are no longer servants, but the friends of God, indeed sons and coheirs with Christ.[25]

THE BOLDNESS OF THE WORSHIPPER

If in such communion of saints our mentored and discipled life has been so enriched by past mentors, it still may be! Our own generation has benefited from such great theologians as Karl Barth, exemplars such as Dietrich Bonhoeffer, and popularizers such as C. S. Lewis. But there is a special quality about my final choice of Hans Urs von Balthasar (1905–1988). As a profound worshipper, he mentors us to be bold in the boldness of God's love. There is a logic in this, for once we have been "delivered out of darkness into His marvelous light," personal assurance grows ever more boldly.

First, von Balthasar exemplified such boldness within the Roman Catholic Church, where he trained as a Jesuit. Before he left the order eighteen years later, he confessed:

> My entire period of study in the Society was a grim struggle with the dreariness of theology, with what men had made out of the glory of revelation. I could not endure this presentation of the word of God … I felt like tearing down with Samson's strength, the whole temple and burying myself beneath the rubble … I wrote "the Apocalypse" with a dogged determination, resolved whatever the cost to rebuilt the world from its foundations.[26]

It was his focus on preparing a commentary on St. John that gave him peace once more, with the comfort of an exacting mentor, Erich Przywara. The community of St. John became likewise his great joy.

First of all, he believed fiercely that one must witness for Christ through one's own sufferings. For the cross must lie at the heart of one's faith. For it was through death and resurrection the disciples were given a new nature, "baptized indeed," "in the name of the Father, the Son, and the Holy Spirit." Significantly, the word *parrhesia*,[27] boldness, is given a new prominence in the Acts of the Apostles, for those faithful witnesses of Christ who like Stephen were martyred for their truthfulness. So the apostle prays, "Grant unto thy servants, that with all boldness they may speak thy word."[28]

In the classical world *parrhesia* had already had a long history. It was the sign of Athenian citizenship for every firstborn male, of civic freedom of speech. It was the aggressive self-confidence of the Cynics. It was expressive of the cosmic world order of the Stoics that made it the wise man's free speech. Later it was, in the Roman world, the candid speech that facilitated friendships.[29] But the New Testament writers no longer interpret *parrhesia* as an issue of human relations, but of the direct result of the gospel to give freedom to approach God, to serve Him, and to love Him with boldness. So Paul asserts, "In Christ I could be bold and order you to do what you ought to do."[30] The writer to the Hebrews speaks of the boldness we have to enter His presence,[31] while John says, "Dear friends, if our hearts do not condemn us, we have confidence before God."[32]

But von Balthasar takes this boldness to a further depth, as being a key word of divine revelation, relating to *"parousia,"* "epiphany," and "glory"—of God's openness to reveal Himself. So, unlike Moses who had to put a veil over his face to hide the fading glory, the Spirit now gives us the new property of "openness" before Christ, to receive the glory of His love.[33] Indeed, in the triune God, His "openness" to us by His Spirit now gives us a new openness to enter into the mysteries of the divine Love.

Thus, second, von Balthasar would encourage us to live the contemplative life as our primary concern. For the Spirit, who alone knows and searches out "the deep things of God," reveals them to those who are "spiritual"—that is, who are open to the Spirit's indwelling. For we have received "the Spirit who is from God, that we may understand what God has freely given us."[34] Thus he concludes that "it is evident that the very possibility of Christian contemplation rests on the doctrine of the Trinity."[35] For this reason, he would encourage us "to pursue a kneeling theology." For prayer is "the only realistic attitude before the revealed mystery."[36]

Third, von Balthasar encourages us to benefit from the "openness of God."[37] For God "is not a sealed fortress to be attacked and seized by our engines of war (in other words, ascetic practices, meditative techniques, and the like), but a house full of open doors through which we are invited to walk. In the divine mystery of the Three-in-One, God's purpose has always been that we, those who are entirely "other," shall participate in the superabundant communion of life. This we can do, for "we enter into the inner being of God through the wounded side of the Father's Son, and Word."[38] Key to this boldness of God in His openness of Being is the mystery of the Trinity, which shapes all this thought and action.

Fourth, we come to the heart of von Balthasar's boldness, indeed what he called in one of his works, *The Heart of the World*.[39] This is the cross, where the nature of God is fully manifest, where Christ stood in our place, "the just for the unjust, so that He might bring us to God."[40] In the context of Auschwitz, where many have assumed "God is dead" or at least absent, von Balthasar brings comfort and assurance. Regarding God "emptying Himself" and becoming our substitution, von Balthasar makes daring use of the distinction between Good Friday and Holy Saturday.[41] It is from "going to the cross" on Good Friday to "going to the dead" on Holy Saturday—indeed the descent into hell, as the ultimate alienation. Yet he insists this self-emptying of Jesus is a Trinitarian act, for the Spirit is still the link between the Father and the Son. This he sees as the "end to theodicy" and thus no longer a question-and-answer of "Where was God at Auschwitz?"

Finally, von Balthasar links the "boldness of God" in fully communicating His love to us in the cross to the responsive "boldness" we are called to live sacrificially for Him. We are discipled above all to live selflessly. For this, prayer becomes indispensable, for once God has called us by name, there is nothing more we can do or be, but to follow Him. There is no alternative, only "Lord, to whom shall we go? You have the words of eternal life."[42] Now all our future has become enfolded in Christ's prayer to His Father:

> "Righteous Father, though the world does not
> know you, I know you, and they know that you
> have sent me. I have made you known to them,
> and will continue to make you known in order
> that the love you have for me may be in them and
> that I myself may be in them."[43]

WORSHIP IS EXPRESSIVE
OF THE CHARACTER OF GOD

The "discipled life," then, of Christians as disciples of Christ is to worship Christ. This is why at the beginning of the spread of Christianity within the Roman Empire, Pliny, a Roman governor and a prudent Stoic, put his finger on the central issue of whether or not to persecute the Christians. For he saw that the Christians' essence was their worship of Christ as God. This was their identifying mark. All that their faith stood for questioned the basis of Roman authority, Stoic reason, and indeed the fabric of their society.[44]

The central mystery of Christian worship still does, for it makes the category of the "person" a theological category and challenges all social theories of the nature of "community." Perhaps tomorrow, beyond the alienation that tends to dominate our present spirit, we may be called upon, ever more critically, to take a central stance upon the same distinctive of our worship as the early Christians.

As Kierkegaard critiqued the three stages of human consciousness, it is God's own character that makes the final judgment. The "Aesthetic" is not the prerogative of the artist, but the bodily form any individual makes of his or her own senses as an "individual," infatuated as one might be by the Greek way of life. The "Beauty" of God confronts such human self-identification by His "Otherness" or holiness—Creator, not creature. Appreciating that "His way is not our way, nor His thoughts our thoughts," both Edwards and Bernard have further helped us explore the uniqueness of God's love.

Likewise, the "Moral" way of life that Stoicism has demonstrated so effectively seems secure in identifying "ideas" of such cardinal virtues with a way of life. But it is still only humanistic, self-contained, oriented entirely to human conditions. It still remains out of touch, observed Kierkegaard, with true Christian conviction "that neither death nor life, nor angels, nor principalities, nor powers, nor things present nor things to come, nor height, nor depth, nor any other creature shall be able to separate us from the love of God, which is in Christ Jesus our Lord."[45] Such a Christian life-view is not merely won from moral experience, as Stoicism would affirm, but is the gift of God's own and abiding presence.

Religion A was for Kierkegaard a form of religious romanticism, which Friedrich Schliermacher had advocated, and so characteristic of his day, just as "civil religion" still is in America today. It makes perfect sense to believe in heaven and in God too. But once God gets too close and challenges us to see how we can "become our own Christian," then religious man is scared away! Then one becomes "Therapeutic" instead, defining the "religious self" in terms of therapeutic health, of "salvation." True religion as Religion B can only become personal and particular when God's love is revealed to be selfless and so enhancing of the "personal." Then we have "saving boldness" as a new and living way of continual worship of the Lamb slain on our behalf.

When we speak then of having "discipled lives," we speak above all of the promise of Jesus to His disciples in the upper room: "I will ask the Father, and he will give you another Counselor [Comforter] to be with you forever—the

Spirit of truth.... I will not leave you as orphans; I will come to you."[46] The fellowship of the Holy Spirit saves us from all loneliness. He gives to each of us "fellowship" with Him,[47] that is, in bringing each "person" into relationship with "the Other." We are therefore never alone, but always "with" the Other. For as the Comforter is together with the Father and the Son, so He is with us to help us, guide us, and truly mentor us. For He "will teach you all things and will remind you of everything,"[48] Jesus promised.

This is our new identity: "the discipled life of Christ." For we have become participators indeed of the triune life of God, to be one in His love.[49] Mentoring may provide us with variable social skills, depending upon the various models we have outlined. But the radical selflessness of Christian discipleship is tested by the nature and quality of our worship. For to give glory to God is both appreciative of our knowledge of God's own being, as well as the freedom from the self to give Him fully ongoing adoration. Only God Himself can truly glorify God by both of these conditions. This is the meaning of our Lord's unique prayer in John 17, when He says, "I have given them the glory that you gave me, that they may be *one as we are one*" (v. 22, emphasis added). So argues Gregory of Nyssa, our last mentor, that it is the Holy Spirit who is the glory between the Father and the Son and who in turn enables us to glorify God in His triune being: "I think that He there in John 17:22 calls the Holy Spirit 'glory,' which He gave to the disciples through His breathing upon them. For there is no other way for those who are divided from one another to be made one if not conjoined by the oneness of the Spirit."[50] Moreover, only the Spirit of God can lead and guide us to appreciate more fully in our worship the character of God as Father, Son, and Holy Spirit.

NOTES

Foreword

1. I owe this analogy to Laurent Daloz, who has several excellent studies on mentoring. See especially, *Mentor: Guiding the Journey of Adult Learners* (San Francisco: Jossey-Bass, 1999).

2. Michael W. Galbraith and Norman H. Cohen, eds., *Mentoring: New Strategies and Challenges* (San Francisco: Jossey-Bass, 1995).

3. See Lois J. Zachary, *The Mentor's Guide: Facilitating Effective Learning Relationships* (San Francisco: Jossey-Bass, 2000). This is a comprehensive introduction with an exhaustive bibliography.

4. Augustine Shutte, *The Mystery of Humanity* (Cape Town, South Africa: Snail Press, 1993), 55.

5. Søren Kierkegaard, *Eighteen Upbuilding Discourses*, eds. and trans. Howard V. Hong and Edna H. Hong (Princeton, NJ: Princeton University Press, 1990), 489.

Chapter 1: Overview: Modern Mentoring and Metaethical Systems

1. Paul Ricoeur, *Oneself as Another*, trans. Kathleen Blamey (Chicago: University of Chicago Press, 1992), 2.

2. James M. Houston, "Why the Contemporary Interest in Mentoring?" *Journal of Christian Education*, vol. 3, no. 1, 1999.

3. Philip Rieff, *The Triumph of the Therapeutic* (New York: Harper & Row, 1966).

4. Angus Reid, *Shakedown* (Toronto: Doubleday, 1996).

5. See Elisabeth Roudinesco, *Jacques Lacan*, trans. Barbara Bray (New York: Columbia University Press, 1997) for Lacan's life and thought.

6. I am indebted for these distinctions to Sister Prudence Allen, *The Concept of Woman: The Aristotelian Revolution, 750 BC–AD 1250* (Grand Rapids: Eerdmans, 1997). They are richly elaborated in her scholarly book.

Chapter 2: The Heroic Myth of Mentor

1. Quoted by C. M. Bowra, *The Greek Experience* (London: Weidenfeld and Nicolson, 1959), 198.

2. See the description of Greek education in Werner Jaeger, *Paideia: The Ideas of Greek Culture, vol. 1*, trans. Gilbert Highet (New York: Galaxy, 1965), 3–14.

3. Ibid., 25.

4. Ibid., 7.

5. Werner, Jaeger, *Early Christianity and Greek Paideia* (Cambridge, MA: Belknap Press of Harvard University Press, 1985, 2–26.

6. Quoted by Bernard Knox in Robert Fagles, trans., *The Odyssey— Homer* (New York: Viking, Penguin Books, 1996), 3. This excellent recent translation of *The Odyssey* is used throughout.

7. Quoted by Ronald Bush, *T. S. Eliot* (New York: Oxford University Press, 1983), 217.

8. Daniel J. Boorstin, *The Creators: A History of Heroes of the Imagination* (New York: Vintage, 1993), 703.

9. Quoted by David G. Richards, *The Hero's Quest for the Self* (Lanham, MD: University Press of America, 1987), 22

10. Pietro Pucci, *Odysseus Polutropus: Intertextual Readings in the Odyssey and the Iliad* (Ithaca, NY: Cornell University Press, 1987), 13–14.

11. Pucci, 16–19. That is to say, Odysseus is the man of many ruses or "polytrophy."

12. Quoted by Hugo Rahner, *Greek Myths and Christian Mystery* (London: Burns and Oates, 1963), 328.

13. *Odyssey*, bk. xix, lines 126–28. p. 394.

14. Homer, *The Odyssey*, bk. 8, lines 198–200, 197.

15. J. R. L. Anderson, *The Ulysses Factor* (London: Hodder & Stoughton, 1970), 197.

16. Cited by Anderson, 29–30.

17. Anderson, 29–30.

18. See. W. B. Stanford, *The Ulysses Theme* (Oxford: Blackwells, 1954).

19. Quoted by Dana S. Gower, "Hero, Healer, and Martyr: Greek Paradigms of the Teacher," *Parabola* 14 (1989), 44.

20. See the recent study by David Blankenhorn, *Fatherless America: Confronting Our Most Urgent Social Problem* (New York: HarperCollins, 1995).

21. François de Fénelon, *Telemachus*, trans. and ed. Patrick Riley (Cambridge, England: Cambridge University Press, 1994).

22. Quoted by E. K. Sanders, *Fénelon and His Friends and Enemies* (London: Green & Co., 1901), 39.

23. Sanders, 161.

24. For the various interpretations given to *Telemachus* see Volker Kapp, *Télémaque de Fénelon* (Tubingen and Paris: Editions Jean Michael: Place, 1982).

25. Analysis of the distinctions is made by Priscilla P. Clark, "The Metamorphoses of Mentor: Fénelon to Balzac," *Romantic Review* 75 (1984), 200–215.

26. Quoted by Sanders, *Fénelon*, 36.

27. Ibid., 358.

28. Ibid., 370.

29. Ibid., 372.

30. Ibid., 373.

31. Ibid., 374.

32. Ibid., 374.

33. Ibid., 376.

34. Ibid., 137.

35. Ibid., 391–92.

36. Ibid., 394.

37. 1 John 2:16 (KJV)

38. Bowra, *The Greek Experience*, 198–99, 201.

Chapter 3: The Stoic as the Moral Mentor

1. Cicero, *Tusculan Disputations*, 3.6.

2. T. S. Eliot, "Shakespeare and the Stoicism of Seneca," in *Selected Essays* (London: Faber & Faber, 1949), 131–32.

3. Eliot, "Shakespeare," 73.

4. Alasdair MacIntyre, *After Virtue*, 2nd. ed. (Notre Dame, IN: University of Notre Dame Press, 1984), 148–49.

5. Hans-Josef Klauck, *The Religious Context of Early Christianity*, trans. Brian McNeil (Edinburgh: T. & T. Clark, 2000), 354–55.

6. Troels Engberg-Pedersen, *The Stoic Theory of Oikeiosis* (Aarhus, Denmark: Aarhus University Press, 1990), 64–71.

7. Engberg-Pedersen, 73.

8. Charles Taylor, *Sources of the Self: The Making of the Modern Identity* (Cambridge, MA: Harvard University Press, 1989), 121.

9. Engberg-Pedersen, Stoic Theory, 181–82.

10. Ibid., 184.

11. Quoted by Martha C. Nussbaum, *The Therapy of Desire* (Princeton, NJ: Princeton University Press, 1994), 326.

12. Nussbaum, *Therapy of Desire*, 351–52.

13. Ibid., 184.

14. Ibid., 101–115.

15. For a good summary of the issue of the emotions in Stoic philosophy, see Julia E. Annas, *Hellenistic Philosophy of Mind* (Berkeley and Los Angeles: University of California Press, 1992), 103–120.

16. For a comparison of Seneca and the apostle Paul, see Jan N. Sevenster, *Paul and Seneca* (Leiden, The Netherlands: E. J. Brill, 1961).

17. Philippians 4:13.

18. 1 Timothy 6:6.

19. David L. Balch, "The Areopagus Speech, an Appeal to the Stoic Historian Posidonius against the Later Stoics and Epicureans," in David Balch, Everett Ferguson, and Wayne Meeks, eds., *Greeks, Romans, and Christians* (Minneapolis: Fortress Press, 1990), 52–79.

20. 1 Corinthians 1:19 (RSV).

21. 1 Corinthians 2:11–16.

22. See the interesting study by Troels Engberg-Pedersen, "Stoicism in Philippians" in his book *Paul in His Hellenistic Context* (Minneapolis: Fortress, 1990), 52–79. Yet he does not sharpen the contrast between Paul and Stoicism as Sevenster does in *Paul and Seneca*.

23. Matthew 19:17; see Gerhard Kittel, ed., *Theological Dictionary of the New Testament* vol. 2 (Grand Rapids: Eerdmans, 1964), vol. 1, 15–17.

24. Ben Witherington III, *Friendship and Fincances in Philippi* (Valley Forge, PA: Trinity Press International, 1994), 115.

25. Abraham J. Malherbe, *Moral Exhortation, a Greco-Roman Sourcebook* (Philadelphia: Westminster, 1986), 41.

26. Philippians 2:6–7.

27. This is well argued by Wayne A. Meeks, *The Origins of Christian Morality: The First Two Centuries* (New Haven and London: Yale University Press, 1993), 86–88.

28. Quoted by Sevenster, *Paul and Seneca*, 107.

29. Quoted by Nussbaum, *Therapy of Desire*, 400.

30. *New International Dictionary of New Testament Theology*, s.v. "joy"; s.v. "rejoice." Also, W. G. Morrice, *Joy in the New Testament* (Grand Rapids: Eerdmans, 1985).

31. Gilbert Meilaender, *The Theory and Practice of Virtue* (Notre Dame, IN: University of Notre Dame Press, 1981), 191.

32. MacIntyre, *After Virtue*, 171.

33. *The New Dictionary of Catholic Spirituality*, s.v. "cardinal virtues," ed. Michael Downey (Collegeville, MN: Liturgical Press, 1993), 114.

34. Quoted by Meilaender, *Theory and Practice of Virtue*, 190.

35. A useful summary of Thomas Aquinas's moral thought is in Romanus Cessario, *The Moral Virtues and Theological Ethics* (Notre Dame, IN: Notre Dame University Press, 1991).

36. Quotations of Aquinas are from Paul J. Waddell, s.v. "virtue" in *The New Dictionary of Catholic Spirituality*, 997–1007.

37. See the schema developed by Kenneth E. Kirk, *Some Principles of Moral Theology and Their Application* (London, New York, Toronto: Longmans, Green & Co., 1930); J. Piepert, *The Four Cardinal Virtues* (Notre Dame, IN: University of Notre Dame Press, 1966), and Cessario, *The Moral Virtues and Theological Ethics*. But since Vatican II, this moral basis for Christian ethics is being more questioned by Catholic moralists.

38. See the critique of Augustine's rationalistic bias in Colin E. Gunton, *The Promise of Trinitarian Theology* (Edinburgh: T. & T. Clark, 1993), 31–57.

39. William Bouwsma, "The Two Faces of Humanism" in *Itinerarium Italicum: The Profile of the Italian Renaissance in the Mirror of Its European Transformations*, eds. Heiko Oberman and Thomas Brady (Leiden, Netherlands: Brill, 1975), 7–9.

40. Quoted by Margo Todd, "Seneca and the Protestant Mind: The Influence of Stoicism on Puritan Ethics," *Archiv fur Reformationesgeschlichte* 74 (1983), 183.

41. However, the mature Calvin in his writings frequently attacked the Stoic doctrine of *apatheia*. See William J. Bouwsma, *John Calvin, a Sixteenth Century Portrait* (Oxford: Oxford University Press, 1988), 133–34. But see also, Egil Grislis, "Seneca and Cicero as Possible Sources of John Calvin's View of Double Predestination," *In Honour of John Calvin 1509–1564,* International Calvin Symposium, ed. E. J. Furcha (Montreal: McGill University Press, 1987), 28–63.

42. Kirk M. Summers, "Theodore Beza's Classical Library and Christian Humanism," *Archiv fur Reformationesgeschlichte* 82 (1991), 193–207; and Alister E. McGrath, *Reformation Thought: An Introduction* (Oxford: Blackwell, 1993), 71–81.

43. Steven Ozment, *The Age of Reform* 1250-1550 (New Haven and London: Yale University Press, 1980), 137.

44. Luther's *Works,* Weimar edition, XLII, Genesis, 470, 333.

45. See Margorie O'Rourke Boyle, "Stoic Luther: Paradoxical Sin and Necessity," *Archiv fur Reformationesgeschlichte* 73 (1992), 69–93.

46. Eliot, "Shakespeare and the Stoicism of Seneca," 132.

47. Marion White Singleton, *God's Courtier: Configuring a Different Grace in George Herbert's "Temple"* (Cambridge: Cambridge University Press, 1987).

48. Michael C. Schoenfeldt, *Prayer and Power: George Herbert and Renaissance Courtship* (Chicago: University of Chicago Press, 1991).

49. See this metaphorical approach in Rosemond Tuve, *A Reading of George Herbert* (Chicago: University of Chicago Press, 1982), 103–111.

50. This and all the following quotations are taken from Alexander B. Grosart, ed. *The Complete Works in Verse and Prose of George Herbert,* vol. 1 (London: Robson and Sons, printed for private circulation, 1874), 164.

51. Quoted by Charles Taylor, *Sources of the Self: The Making of the Modern Identity* (Cambridge, MA: Harvard University Press, 1989), 147.

52. Ibid., 153.

53. William Barrett, *Death of the Soul: From Descartes to the Computer* (New York: Anchor, Doubleday, 1986).

54. Robert W. Jenson, *America's Theologian: A Recommendation of Jonathan Edwards* (New York: Oxford University Press, 1988), 77.

55. Jonathan Edwards, "The Nature of True Virtue," ed. Paul Ramsey, in *Jonathan Edwards: Ethical Writings* (New Haven and London: Yale University Press, 1989), 537–619.

56. Ibid., 141.

57. J. M. Sherwood, ed., *Memoirs of Rev. David Brainerd* (New York: Funk & Wagnall, 1884). Sherwood quotes from the original edition.

58. Sermon preached at Brainerd's funeral, Oct. 12, 1747, quoted by Sherwood, 348.

59. See Marcus L. Loane, *They Were Pilgrims* (Blackwood, Australia: New Creation Publications, 1985), for a collective study of these men, together with that of Keith Falconer.

60. Andrew M. Bonar, *Memoir and Remains of Murray M'Cheyne* (Grand Rapids: Baker, 1978), 37.

Chapter 4: The Secular Psychotherapeutic Mentor

1. Christopher Lasch, *The Culture of Narcissism* (New York: W. W. Norton, 1978), 7.

2. See Karl Menninger, *Whatever Became of Sin?* (New York: Hawthorn Books, 1973).

3. John MacMurray, *The Structure of Religious Experience* (New Haven: Yale University Press, 1971), 24; *Religion, Art and Science* (Liverpool: Liverpool University Press, 1961), 57–58.

4. *Encyclopaedia Britannica,* 14th ed., s.v. "John Locke."

5. Robert W. Jenson, *America's Theologian: A Recommendation of Jonathan Edwards* (New York and Oxford: Oxford University Press, 1988), 9.

6. D. Shakow and D. Rapaport, *The Influence of Freud on American Psychology,* vol. 4, Monograph 13, *Psychological Issues* (New York: International University Press, 1964), 95.

7. See Paul Ricoeur, *Figuring the Sacred Religion Narrative and Imagination,* trans. David Pellauer (Minneapolis: Fortress Press. 1995).

8. Quoted by Philip Cushman, *Constructing the Self, Constructing America* (Boston: Addison-Wesley, 1995), 114.

9. Martha C. Nussbaum, *The Therapy of Desire* (Princeton, NJ: Princeton University Press, 1994), 133–35.

10. Cushman, *Constructing the Self,* 115.

11. Quoted by Ethan Watters and Richard Ofshe, *Therapy's Delusions* (New York: Scribner, 1999), 87.

12. Watters and Ofshe, *Therapy's Delusion*, 86.

13. W. H. Auden, "In Memory of Sigmund Freud," in *Collected Short Poems* (London: Faber & Faber, 1950).

14. June Singer, "Jung's Gnosticism and Contemporary Gnosis" in *Jung's Challenge to Contemporary Religion,* eds. Murray Stein and Robert L. Moore (Wilmette, IL: Chiron, 1987), 73–91.

15. Jeffrey M. Masson, *The Assault on Truth: Freud's Suppression of the Seduction Theory* (New York: Farrar, Strauss, & Giroux, 1984); James Hillman and Michael Ventura, *A Hundred Years of Therapy and the World Is Getting Worse* (New York: Farrar, Strauss & Giroux, 1985).

16. Richard Webster, *Why Freud Was Wrong* (New York: HarperCollins, 1995), 402–434.

17. Ernest Gellner, *The Psychoanalytic Movement* (Evanston, IL: Northwestern University Press, 1996).

18. Marshall Edelson, *Hypothesis and Evidence in Psychoanalysis* (Chicago: University of Chicago Press, 1984).

19. *A Dictionary of the Social Sciences,* s.v. "projections," eds. Julian Gould and William Kolb (London: Tavistock Publications, 1964), 545–46.

20. J. Holms and R. Lindley, *The Values of Psychotherapy* (Oxford: Oxford University Press, 1989), 127.

21. M. and A. Balint, "On Transference and Counter-Transference," in *Primary Love, and Psycho-analytic Techniques,* ed. M. Balint (New York: Liveright, 1965).

22. Quoted in Anthony Storr, *Freud* (Oxford: Oxford University Press, 1994), 127.

23. Sigmund Freud, "The Ego and the Id," *Collected Works* vol. 22 (London: Hogarth Press, 1940).

24. Freud, *Collected Works*, vol. 19, 26.

25. Freud, *Collected Works*, vol. XIV, 90. See also Storr, 56.

26. Freud, *Collected Works*, vol. IV, xxxii.

27. Freud, *Collected Works*, vol. V, 608.

28. Storr, *Freud,* 37.

29. Rieff, *Triumph of the Therapeutic,* 91.

30. Stein and Moore, eds., *Jung's Challenge to Contemporary Religion.* Their work has essays illustrative of the allurement. See also Morton

Kelsey, *Christo-Psychology* (New York: Crossroad, 1982), 153–54, who "thanks the Lord of life for his servant Jung."

31. Reiff, *Triumph*, 87.

32. See Richard Noll, *The Jung Cult* (Princeton, NJ: Princeton University Press, 1994), 75–138.

33. Webster, *Why Freud Was Wrong*, 383.

34. Quoted by John Kerr, *A Most Dangerous Method* (New York: Sinclair Stevenson, 1999), 317–18.

35. Ernesto Spinelli, *Demystifying Therapy* (London: Constable, 1994), 25.

36. Gellner, *Psychoanalytic Movement*.

37. D. W. Winnicott, *The Maturational Process and the Facilitating Environment* (London: Hogarth Press, 1965).

38. John Bowlby, *Child Care and the Growth of Love* (London: Pelican Books, 1950).

39. Margaret Mahler, *The Psychological Birth of the Human Infant* (New York: Basic Books, 1975).

40. Heinz Kohut, "The Psychoanalytic Treatment of the Narcissistic Personality Disorder," in *The Search for the Self*, ed. P. H. Ornstein (New York: International Universities Press, 1968), vol. 1, 506–7.

41. Spinelli, *Demystifying Therapy*, 255–78.

42. Ibid., 268.

43. See J. D. Frank and J. B. Frank, *Persuasion and Healing: A Comparative Study of Psychotherapy*, 3rd ed. (Baltimore: Johns Hopkins University Press, 1991).

44. Cushman, *Constructing the Self*, 214–15.

45. Ibid., 32–35.

46. René Girard, *Descartes, Desire, and the Novel* (Baltimore: Johns Hopkins University Press, 1963), 61.

47. Eugene Webb, *The Self Between* (Seattle, WA: University of Washington Press, 1993), 24.

48. François Roustang, *Psychoanalysis Never Lets Go*, trans. Ned Lukacher (Baltimore, MD: John Hopkins University Press, 1983), 14.

49. Nicholas Rand and Maria Torok, *Questions for Freud* (Cambridge, MA: Harvard University Press, 1993), 224.

50. Quoted by Thomas C. Oden, *Parables of Kierkegaard* (Princeton, NJ: Princeton University Press, 1978), 50.

Chapter 5: Mentored and Discipled for Christian Living

1. In Euripides' play *Medea,* love is portrayed as having snakes in her familiars, and so Stoics like Seneca advised against marriage being treated erotically. This is, of course, a pagan, not a Christian, interpretation of love. But for Augustine, Bernard of Clairvaux, and other Christian writers, love is the greatest expression of reality, certainly more than philosophical knowledge.

2. Bruce H. Kirmmse, ed., *Encounters with Kierkegaard: A Life as Seen by His Contemporaries* (Princeton, NJ: Princeton University Press, 1996), 98.

3. Howard V. Hong and Edna H. Hong, eds., and trans., *Søren Kierkegaard's Journals and Papers,* vol. 1 (Bloomington, IN: Indiana University Press, 1967), xxviii.

4. Robert C. Roberts, "Kierkegaard, Wittgenstein, and a Method of 'Virtue Ethics,'" *Kierkegaard in Post/Modernity,* ed. Martin J. Matustik and Merold Westphal (Bloomington, IN: Indiana University Press, 1995), 142–66.

5. O. Hobart Mowrer, *Learning Theory and Personal Dynamics* (New York: Ronald Press, 1980), 541.

6. Quoted in George Connell, *To Be One Thing: Personal Unity in Kierkegaard's Thought* (Macon, GA: Mercer University Press, 1985), 9.

7. See summary in Peter Vardy, *Kierkegaard* (London: Fount, HarperCollins, 1996), 22–33.

8. Arnold B. Come, *Kierkegaard as Theologian: Recovering My Self* (Montreal: McGill-Queen's University Press, 1997), 16.

9. Kierkegaard, *Journals and Papers,* 3023, xi (1854).

10. David J. Gouwens, *Kierkegaard as Religious Thinker* (Cambridge: Cambridge University Press, 1996), 5.

11. Søren Kierkegaard, *Fear and Trembling and Sickness unto Death,* trans. Walter Lowrie (Princeton, NJ: Princeton University Press, 1974), 30.

12. Kierkegaard, *Journals and Papers,* vol. 1, 448.

13. Ibid., 85.

14. See James W. Jones, *Contemporary Psychoanalysis and Religion* (New Haven and London: Yale University Press, 1991); and Charles

Bollas, *Being a Character: Psychoanalysis and Self Experience* (New York: Hill and Wang, 1992).

15. Kierkegaard, *Sickness unto Death,* 14.

16. Søren Kierkegaard, *Attack upon Christendom,* trans. Walter Lowrie (Princeton, NJ: Princeton University Press, 1968), 159.

17. Kierkegaard, *Sickness unto Death,* 82.

18. C. Stephen Evans, "Kierkegaard's View of the Unconscious," in *Kierkegaard in Post/Modernity,* eds. Martin J. Matustik and Merold Westphal (Bloomington, IN: Indiana University Press, 1995), 78.

19. John W. Elrod, "The Social Dimension of Despair," in Robert L. Perkins, ed., *International Kierkegaard Commentary: Sickness unto Death* (Macon, GA: Mercer University Press, 1987), 107.

20. Quoted by Come, *Kierkegaard as Theologian,* 135.

21. See Valerie Saiving, "The Human Situation: A Feminine View," *The Journal of Religion* 40 (April 1960), 100–112; also Carol Gilligan, *In a Different Voice: Psychological Theory and Women's Development* (Cambridge, MA: Cambridge University Press, 1982).

22. See the excellent essay of William J. Cahoy, "One Species or Two? Kierkegaard's Anthropology and the Feminist Critique of the Concept of Sin," *Modern Theology* (October 1995), 429–54.

23. Kierkegaard, *Journals and Papers,* vol. 1, 346.

24. Ibid., 347.

25. Ibid., 349.

26. Come, *Kierkegaard as Humanist,* 49.

27. Ibid., 61.

28. Søren Kierkegaard, *Either/Or,* trans. Walter Lowrie (1974: reprint, Princeton, NJ: Princeton University Press, 1987), 193.

29. Søren Kierkegaard, *Fear and Trembling* and *The Sickness unto Death,* trans. Alistair Hannay (London: Penguin, 1985), 96.

30. Søren Kierkegaard, *The Concept of Anxiety,* ed. Reidar Thomte (Princeton, NJ: Princeton University Press, 1980), 115–16.

31. T. S. Eliot, *The Complete Poems and Plays of T. S. Eliot* (London: Faber & Faber, 1969), 413–16.

32. Eliot, 162.

33. Kierkegaard, *The Sickness unto Death,* 214, 216, 218.

34. Quoted by Come, *Kierkegaard as Humanist,* 254.

35. Come, *Kierkegaard as Theologian,* 254, 277.

36. Ibid., 15.

37. Kierkegaard, *Fear and Trembling,* trans. Howard V. Hong and Edna H. Hong (Princeton, NJ: Princeton University Press, 1980), xi.

38. There are many commentaries on the three stages. A lucid introduction is given by Peter Vardy, *Kierkegaard* (London: Harper Collins, Fount Paperback, 1996), 34–63; it is elaborated by George Connell, *To Be One Thing: Personal Unity in Kierkegaard's Thought* (Macon, GA: Mercer University Press, 1985); see also C. Stephen Evans, *Kierkegaard's Fragments and Postscript* (Atlantic Highlands, NJ: Humanities Press International, 1989), 33–54.

39. John D. Glenn, "The Definition of the Self" in *International Kierkegaard Commentary: The Sickness unto Death,* ed. Robert L. Perkins (Macon, GA: Mercer University Press, 1987), 31–38. See also Harold Westphal, "Kierkegaard's Psychology and Unconscious Despair," *International Kierkegaard Commentary,* 39–66.

40. Robert L. Perkins, ed., *International Commentary on The Sickness Unto Death,* vol. 19, (Macon, GA: Mercer University Press, 1987), 140.

41. On the religious unity and upbuilding of humanity see Gouwens, *Kierkegaard as Religious Thinker,* 93–121.

42. See C. Stephen Evans, "Kierkegaard's View of the Unconscious" in Matustik and Westphal, *Kierkegaard in Post/Modernity,* 76–97.

43. John Owen, *Sin and Temptation,* ed. James M. Houston (Minneapolis: Bethany, 1996).

44. Quoted by Evans, "Kierkegaard's View of the Unconscious," 77.

45. Søren Kierkegaard, *Purity of Heart Is to Will One Thing,* trans. Douglas V. Steere (New York: Harper & Row, 1956), 31.

Chapter 6: Discipled to Be Persons in Christ

1. John D. Zizioulas, "The Doctrine of the Holy Trinity," in *Trinitarian Theology Today,* ed. Christoph Schwobel (Edinburgh: T. & T. Clark, 1995), 58, 59.

2. Jacques Derrida, *Politics of Friendship,* trans. George Collins (London: Verso, 1997), 222.

3. Derrida, *Politics of Friendship,* 24.

4. Søren Kierkegaard, *The Sickness unto Death,* trans. Walter Lowrie (Princeton, NJ: Princeton University Press, 1974), 147.

5. Marcel Maurs, "A Category of the Human Mind: The Notion of Person; The Notion of Self," in *The Category of the Person,* eds. Michael Carruthers, Steven Collins, Steven Lukes (Cambridge, MA, and New York: Cambridge University Press, 1991), 14–16.

6. For an extensive discussion of this subject, see M. Nedoncelle, "Prosopon et Persona dans l'Antiquite Classique," *Revue des Sciences Religeuses,* Strasbourge, vol. 22 (1948), 277–99.

7. Robert Fagles, trans., *The Odyssey* (New York: Viking, Penguin Books, 1996), bk. 1, 195-197, 88.

8. See the excellent study of Colin E. Gunton, *The One, the Three and the Many* (Cambridge, MA: Cambridge University Press, 1993).

9. The nuance of concrete individuality is first found in Cicero. See John D. Zizioulas, *Being as Communion* (Crestwood, NY: St. Vladimir's Seminary Press, 1985), 35, note 21.

10. Amelie Oksenberg Rorty, "A Literary Postscript" in the *The Identities of Persons* (Berkeley: University of California Press, 1976), 309.

11. For example, see Gordon Allport, *The Person in Psychology* (Boston: Beacon Press, 1968); Dan P. McAdams, *The Person: An Introduction to Personality Psychology* (San Diego: Harcourt Brace Jovanovich, 1989); Charles Taylor, *Sources of the Self* (Cambridge, MA: Harvard University Press, 1989).

12. C. S. Lewis, *The Abolition of Man* (London: Collins, 1955).

13. Clifford Langley, "Sacred and Profane," *The Daily Telegraph,* January 16, 1994, 25.

14. David Jenkins, *The Glory of Man* (London: SCM Press, 1969), 95–96.

15. See Anthony Giddens, *Modernity and Self-Identity: Self and Society in the Late Modern Age* (Stanford, CA: Stanford University Press, 1991), especially chap. 6.

16. Betty Friedan, *The Feminine Mystique* (Harmondsworth, England: Penguin Books, 1965), 61.

17. Carl Rogers, *On Becoming a Person* (Boston: Houghton Mifflin, 1961), 108, 110, 273. See the similar critique in Stephen Pattison, *A Critique of Pastoral Care* (London: SCM Press, 1988).

18. Christopher Lasch, *The Minimal Self: Psychic Survival in Troubled Times* (New York: Norton, 1984), 16.

19. Jean-François Lyotard, *The Inhuman,* trans. Geoffrey Bennington and Rachel Bowlby (Stanford, CA: Stanford University Press, 1991), 2–5.

20. Matthew 18:3.

21. Lyotard, *Inhuman,* 1–7.

22. Raul Ricoeur, *Oneself as Another,* trans. Kathleen Blamey (Chicago: Chicago University Press, 1992), 302.

23. As a Christian psychologist, Paul Vitz has made a comparable contrast in *Man and Mind: A Christian Theory of Personality* (Hillsdale, MI: Hillsdale College Press, 1987), 199–220.

24. Julius Gould and William L. Kolb, eds., *A Dictionary of the Social Sciences* (London: Tavistock Publications, 1964).

25. See for example, Rorty, *Identity of Persons;* Allport, *Person in Psychology;* and McAdams, *Introduction to Personality Psychology.*

26. See the important essays in Christoph Schwöbel and Colin E. Gunton, eds., *Persons, Divine and Human* (Edinburgh: T. & T. Clark, 1991).

27. Of the numerous theological references to the *imago Dei,* an illuminating summary is in Otto Weber, *Foundations of Dogmatics,* vol. 1, trans. Darrell L. Gruder (Grand Rapids: Eerdmans, 1981), 558–79.

28. Eberhard Jungel, "On Becoming Truly Human," in *Theological Essays* II, trans. Arnold Neufeldt-Fast and J. B. Webster (Edinburgh: T. & T. Clark, 1995), 216–40.

29. Quoted by Colin E. Gunton, *God and Freedom* (Edinburgh: T. & T. Clark, 1995), 80.

30. Alistair McFadyen, *The Call to Personhood* (Cambridge, England: Cambridge University Press, 1990), 48–61.

31. See Eberhard Jungel, "Humanity in Correspondence to God," in *Theological Essays,* vol. 1, trans. J. B. Webster (Edinburgh: T. & T. Clark, 1989), 124–45.

32. 2 Corinthians 5:17–18.

33. Steven Lukes, *Individualism* (Oxford: Basil Blackwell, 1973), 3–26.

34. Richard N. Longenecker, ed., *Patterns of Discipleship in the New Testament* (Grand Rapids: Eerdmans, 1996), 145.

35. Martin Hengel, *The Charismatic Leader and His Followers,* trans. J. Greig (New York: Crossroad, 1981).

36. Ernest Best, *Disciples and Discipleship: Studies in the Gospel According to Mark* (Edinburgh: T. & T. Clark, 1986).

37. Michael J. Wilkins, *The Concept of Disciple in Matthew's Gospel* (Leiden, The Netherlands: Brill, 1988).

38. Joseph A. Fitzmyer, "Discipleship in the Lucan Writings," in *Luke the Theologian: Aspects of His Teaching* (New York: Paulist Press, 1989), 117–45.

39. R. Alan Culpepper, *The Johannine School* (Missoula, MT: Scholars Press, 1975).

40. See the collection of essays in Longenecker, *Patterns of Discipleship.*

41. Matthew 19:21.

42. See the excellent critique given by John M. Lozano, C.M.F., *Discipleship: Towards an Understanding of Religious Life,* vol. 2, trans. Beatrice Wilczynski (Chicago: Claret Center for Resources in Spirituality, 1983), 1–72, 259–300.

43. Lozano, *Discipleship,* 71.

44. 1 Corinthians 15:10.

45. This is affirmed in a standard textbook, Gerard Egan, *The Skilled Helper* (Pacific Grove, CA: Brooks/Cole, 1990), 117.

46. See the elaboration of these themes in Dietrich von Hildebrand, *Transformation in Christ* (Manchester, NH: Sophia Institute Press, 1974), 3–104.

47. Søren Kierkegaard, *Works of Love,* eds. and trans. Howard V. Hong and Edna H. Hong (New York: Harper, 1967), 58–72.

48. John 17:11, 26.

49. Quoted by John Cumming, *Letters from Saints to Sinners* (New York: Crossroad, 1996), 9.

50. Acts 20:28.

51. Grace Perigo, trans., *The Letters of Adam of Perseigne,* vol. 1 (Kalamazoo, MI: Cistercian Publications, 1976), 54–55.

52. Perigo, *Letters of Adam,* 67.

53. John Leinenweber, ed., *Letters of Saint Augustine* (Terrytown, NY: Triumph Books, 1992), 82.

54. Quoted from Cumming, *Saints to Sinners,* 134–35.

55. Ibid., 70.

56. Ibid., 59–60.

57. Dietrich Bonhoeffer, *Letters and Papers from Prison,* ed. Eberhard Bethge, trans. Reginald H. Fuller (London: SCM, 1953).

58. Quoted by Cumming, *Saints to Sinners,* 223–24.

59. Bruno Scott James, trans., *The Letters of St. Bernard of Clairvaux* (Kalamazoo, MI: Cistercian Publications, 1998), 134–35.

60. James, *Letters of St. Bernard,* 296.

61. Theodore G. Trappert, ed. and trans., *Luther: Letters of Spiritual Counsel* (Vancouver: Regent College Publishing, 1997), 82.

62. C. S. Lewis, *Letters of C. S. Lewis*, ed. Walter Hooper (London: Collins, 1966), 423.

63. Lewis, 431.

64. Henri de Tourville, *Letters of Direction*, intro. Evelyn Underhill (London: Mowbray, 1982), 91–94.

Chapter 7: Discipled by the Word of God

1. Hong, *Søren Kierkegaard's Journals and Papers*, 40–41.

2. John Calvin, *Institutes of the Christian Religion*, ed. John T. McNeill, from *The Library of Christian Classics*, eds. John Baillie, John T. McNeill, and Henry P. Van Dusen (Philadelphia: Westminster Press, 1960), 1.18.

3. Søren Kierkegaard, *The Sickness unto Death*, eds. Howard V. Hong and Edna H. Hong (Princeton, NJ: Princeton University Press, 1980), 30.

4. See the significant historical survey in Pierre Courcelle, *Connais-tu, Toi Meme, de Socrate à Saint Bernard* (Paris: Etudes Augustiniennes, 1975).

5. Hans Dieter Betz, "The Delphic Adage in Hermetic Interpretation," *Harvard Theological Review* 63 (October 1970), 465–84.

6. Søren Kierkegaard, *For Self-Examination: Judge for Yourself!*, eds. and trans. Howard V. Hong and Edna H. Hong (Princeton, NJ: Princeton University Press, 1990), 25.

7. Ibid., 35–36.

8. Quoted by Come, *Kierkegaard as Theologian*, 254.

9. Ibid., 44.

10. Jean-Luc Marion, *God Without Being*, trans. Thomas A. Carlson (Chicago: University of Chicago Press, 1995), 9–24.

11. Kevin J. Vanhoozer, *Is There a Meaning in This Text?* (Grand Rapids: Zondervan, 1998), 460.

12. Marion, *God Without Being*, 19.

13. Kierkegaard, *Sickness unto Death,* 30.

14. See the excellent study of Timothy Houston Polk, *The Biblical Kierkegaard: Reading by the Rule of Faith* (Macon, GA: Mercer University Press, 1997), 54–60.

15. Robert W. Jenson, "Hermeneutics and the Life of the Church," in C. Braaten, ed., *Reclaiming the Bible for the Church* (Grand Rapids: Eerdmans, 1995), 89–105.

16. Stephen D. Moore, *Literary Criticism and the Gospels: The Theoretical Challenge* (New Haven: Yale University Press, 1989), 66.

17. Klaus Bockmuehl, *Listening to the God Who Speaks* (Colorado Springs, CO: Helmers and Howard, 1990).

18. Polk, *Biblical Kierkegaard,* 36–39.

19. Ibid., 68–69.

20. Jenson, "Hermeneutics and the Life of the Church," 89–105.

21. John A. Darr, *On Character-Building: The Reader and the Rhetoric of Characterization in Luke-Acts* (Louisville: Westminster, 1992), 55.

22. James D. G. Dunn, *The Living Word* (Philadelphia: Fortress, 1988), 119.

23. George Steiner, *Real Presences* (Chicago: University of Chicago Press, 1989), 96.

24. Paul Beauchamp, *Creation et separation: Etude exegetique du chapitre premier de Genese* (Paris: Desclee de Brouwer, 1970), quoted in Jacques Ellul, *The Humiliation of the Word* (Grand Rapids: Eerdmans, 1985), 64.

25. See the excellent study by Susan A. Handelman, *The Slayers of Moses* (Albany, NY: State University of New York Press, 1982), especially chap. 8, "The Critic as Kabbalist," 179–223.

26. Ellul, *The Humiliation of the Word,* 65.

27. James M. Houston, *I Believe in the Creator* (Grand Rapids: Eerdmans, 1978), 49–56.

28. Hebrews 1:1.

29. Brevard S. Childs, "The Rationale of a Canonical Approach," in *The New Testament as Canon: An Introduction* (Philadelphia: Fortress Press, 1984), 34–47. Also, the essays in Gene Tucker, David Petersen, and Robert Wilson, eds., *Canon, Theology, and Old Testament Interpretation: Essays in Honor of Brevard S. Childs* (Philadelphia: Fortress Press, 1988).

30. Kierkegaard, *For Self-Examination,* 55.

31. See N. T. Wright, *The New Testament and the People of God* (Minneapolis: Fortress Press, 1992), 245.

32. Walter Brueggemann, *The Creative Word: Canon as a Model for Biblical Education* (Philadelphia: Fortress Press, 1989).

33. Brevard S. Childs, *Memory and Tradition in Israel* (London: SCM Press, 1962), 88.

34. Deuteronomy 6:4-5.

35. Deuteronomy 8:5-6 (NRSV).

36. See Bruce K. Waltke, "The Fear of the Lord: The Foundation for a Relationship with God," in *Alive to God*, eds. J. I. Packer and Loren Wilkinson (Downers Grove, IL: InterVarsity, 1992), 17–33.

37. Amos 4:4; see also 5:4-6.

38. Micah 6:8.

39. Harry Gersh, *The Sacred Books of the Jews* (New York: Stein and Day, 1972), 68.

40. Job 28:12 (NASB).

41. Psalm 31:14-15 (NASB).

42. Luke 4:21.

43. 1 Corinthians 1:23.

44. See the lucid interpretation given by Ben Witherington III, *Jesus the Sage: The Pilgrimage of Wisdom* (Minneapolis: Fortress Press, 1994).

45. See the massive and illuminating volumes of N. T. Wright, *Christian Origins and the Question of God*, vol. 2, *Jesus and the Victory of God* (Minneapolis: Fortress Press, 1996), 147–97.

46. N. T. Wright, *Christian Origins and the Question of God*, vol. 1, *The New Testament and the People of God* (Minneapolis: Fortress press, 1992).

47. Matthew 5:17.

48. N. T. Wright, *The Climax of the Covenant: Christ and the Law in Pauline Theology* (Minneapolis: Fortress Press, 1993).

49. Augustine, *Confessions,* 5.14, trans. Henry Chadwick (Oxford: Oxford University Press, 1991), 88.

50. 2 Corinthians 3:6.

51. 1 Corinthians 2:10-16.

52. See 1 Corinthians 12:4-13.

53. Quoted by Hans W. Frei, *The Eclipse of Biblical Narrative* (New Haven: Yale University Press, 1974), 3.

54. Acts. 17:28.

55. Romans 10:1, 4.

56. Romans 10:6-11.

57. Douglas J. Moo, *The Epistle to the Romans* (Grand Rapids: Eerdmans, 1996), 653–57. See also the excellent discussion on the whole passage in Richard B. Hays, *Echoes of Scripture in the Letters of Paul* (New Haven: Yale University Press, 1989), 73–83.

58. Psalm 119:151 (NASB).

59. See Brueggemann, *The Creative Word,* 92–102.

60. 2 Kings 19:15, 19 (NASB).

61. Quoted in Ford Lewis Battles, ed. and trans., *The Piety of John Calvin* (Grand Rapids: Baker, 1978), 27–28.

62. Psalm 119:105.

63. See Galatians 5:25.

64. 2 Corinthians 12:9.

65. This is a paraphrase of 1 Corinthians 15:8 given by Dr. Martin Lloyd-Jones.

66. Interpretative paraphrase of 2 Corinthians 12:9b given by Marva Dawn, *Joy in Weakness* (St. Louis: Concordia, 1994), 132.

Chapter 8: Discipled for Worship in Community

1. Stephen Sykes, *The Identity of Christianity* (Philadelphia: Fortress Press, 1984), 269.

2. Revelation 1:4; see also 4:8.

3. See Revelation 1:4; 5:12; 7:9-10.

4. John 4:24.

5. Richard Bauckham, *The Theology of the Book of Revelation* (Cambridge, England: Cambridge University Press, 1993), 162.

6. J. J. Collins, "Introduction: Towards the Morphology of a Genre," *Semeia* 14 (1979), 9.

7. Mark 7:6.

8. Bruce W. Longenecker, *The Triumph of Abraham's God: The Transformation of Identity in Galatians* (Nashville: Abingdon, 1998), 185.

9. Hans Mol, *Identity and the Sacred* (Oxford: Blackwell, 1976), 11.

10. Zechariah 2:10–11.

11. Revelation 21:23–26.

12. Jonathan Edwards, *Religious Affections* ed. John E. Smith (New Haven: Yale University Press, 1959), 135–36.

13. Søren Kierkegaard, *Concluding Unscientific Postscript,* ed. David F. Swenson (Princeton, NJ: Princeton University Press, 1941), 337–81.

14. Edwards, *Religious Affections,* 103.

15. Bernard of Clairvaux, *On the Song of Songs,* vol. 1, Sermons 1-20, trans. Kilian Walsh (Kalamazoo, MI: Cistercian Publications, 1981), 16.

16. P. Verdeyen, "Un Theologien de L'Experience," in *Bernard de*

Clairvaux: Histoire, mentalites, spiritualité: colloque de Lyons-Citeaux-Dijon (Paris: Editions du Cerf, 1992), 559.

17. Bernard of Clairvaux, *Advent Sermon*, 5, 1, 561.

18. Bernard of Clairvaux, *On the Song of Songs*, vol. 4, Sermon 74, trans. Irene Edmonds (Kalamazoo, MI: Cistercian Publications, 1980), 87.

19. Bernard of Clairvaux, *On the Song of Songs*, vol. 1, Sermon 8, 1.

20. See the authoritative study of Michael Casey, *A Thirst for God: Spiritual Desire in Bernard of Clairvaux's Sermons on the Song of Songs* (Kalamazoo, MI: Cistercian Publications, 1988).

21. Bernard of Clairvaux, *On the Song of Songs*, vol. 1, Sermon 18, 6.

22. Bernard of Clairvaux, vol. 4, Sermon 83, 6.

23. Bernard of Clairvaux, *On Loving God*, 9.26 (Kalamazoo, MI: Cistercian Publications, 1995).

24. Ibid., 9.26.

25. As a helpful commentary on his treatise see Emero Stiegman, *Bernard of Clairvaux: An Analytical Commentary* (Kalamazoo, MI: Cistercian Publications, 1995); also Dennis E. Tamburello, *Bernard of Clairvaux: Essential Writings* (New York: Crossroad, 2000), 85–103.

26. Quoted by Peter Henrici, "Hans Urs von Balthasar," in *Communio* (Fall 1989), 313.

27. Von Balthasar notes it is derived from *pan* ("all") and *rhe* (root for "to speak"), hence fullness of speech.

28. Acts 4:29 (KJV).

29. See the essays in John T. Fitzgerald, ed., *Friendship, Flattery, and Frankness of Speech* (Leiden, Netherlands: E. J. Brill, 1996).

30. Philemon 8.

31. See Hebrews 3:6, 14; 4:16; 10:22.

32. 1 John 3:21.

33. See 2 Corinthians 3:12–18.

34. 1 Corinthians 2:12.

35. Hans Urs von Balthasar, *On Prayer*, trans. A. V. Littledale (London: SPCK, 1973), 62.

36. Antonio Sicari, "Hans Urs von Balthasar: Theology and Holiness," *Communio* (Fall 1989), 362.

37. Hans Urs von Balthasar, *Mysterium Paschale: The Mystery of Easter*, trans. Aidan Nichols, (Edinburgh: T. & T. Clark, 1990), 148–81.

38. Von Balthasar, *On Prayer*, 62.

39. Hans Urs von Balthasar, *The Heart of the World,* trans. Erasmo S. Leiva (San Francisco: Ignatius Press, 1979).

40. 1 Peter 3:18 (NASB).

41. Von Balthasar, *Mysterium Paschale,* 89–188.

42. John 6:68.

43. John 17:25–26.

44. Robert L. Wilken, *The Christians as the Romans Saw Them* (New Haven: Yale University Press, 1984), 1–30.

45. Quoted by Alastair Hannay, *Kierkegaard: A Biography* (Cambridge, England: Cambridge University Press, 2001), 109.

46. John 14:16–18.

47. See 2 Corinthians 13:14; Philippians 2:1.

48. John 14:26.

49. See 2 Peter 1:4.

50. Quoted by Paul M. Quay, *The Mystery Hidden for Ages in God* (New York: Peter Lang, 1995), 33.

GLOSSARY

Aesthetic—In Søren Kierkegaard's thought, this category of self-hood is dedicated only to the values of constructing one's own identity, regardless of the ethical norms of society. This is achieved either through living in the world of one's own ideas or through the pursuit of pleasure, even sophisticated interpretations of pleasure. This can be the pursuit of money or power, or reputation, or even hobbies—indeed, anything that preoccupies the pursuit of temporal things. The Heroic is simply one example of this class of pursuits.

Antinominian (Greek *anti*, against; *nomos*, law)—Doctrine according to which Christians are free from the law. Gnostic heretics in the early church abused the use of the law by interpreting it as freedom for license. Anabaptists were accused of it by the other Reformers, as were the Independents later. The Wesleyan movement produced its own antinomians, who claimed an inner experience, as did Quakers and other church separatists. So it tends to be an approach to salvation that emphasizes the individual's faith rather than following ecclesial rules.

Apatheia (Greek, *a*, without; *pathe*, emotions and passions)— Living without emotions was first advocated by Zeno, but later Stoics like Seneca sought rather for balance of the emotions. The Desert Fathers took the discipline of the passions much more severely, and the Eastern church has always tended in its monastic tradition to idealize this concept of detachment from the passions.

Aretê—In classical Greek culture, the pursuit of excellence. *Aretê* reflected the special worth of humans before the gods. By reaching human potential, or one's own capacities, people were fulfilling their *telos,* or goal, which was "good," and even "godly." Thus most things that a human being could admire and esteem were included within the category of *aretê*. But *aretê* was not open to all: Freedom was a prerequisite, which meant slaves could not achieve it, so it really pertained to the training of the elite.

Aristotelian—Having to do with the teachings of Aristotle (384–322 BC), which emphasized empirical and descriptive analysis of the subject. Its emphasis has remained expressive of its constituent parts and their relation to the whole without reference to its historical genesis or extrinsic moral values. It is a frame of mind prevalent today.

Augustinianism—Expressive of the teachings of Augustine (354–430), who taught that a spiritual traveler (*homo viator*) finds his or her home in God and a joy of intimacy in the triune God, and that he or she can appreciate all creation as God's goodness. Daily living is to be expressed in the gift of

God's love, or *caritas*. Created in the image of God, the Christian is ever seeking, in humility and loving intimacy with God, to grow in sanctifying grace. By the practical Rule of Augustine, he intended for Christian communities to live in brotherly love. He was particularly vigilant against the followers of Pelagius, who belittled sin and claimed an independent role for human self-effort.

Bibliolatry—Reading the Bible for self-serving purposes, as a form of idolatry, using it for self-promotion instead of reading it iconically, as referring to the God of biblical revelation.

Canon (Greek *kanon*, measuring rod)—Refers to a list of recommended or authoritative books. Within this biblical framework, the canon of the Old and New Testaments encloses an area of texts deemed authoritative of God's revelation to His people.

Cardinal virtues (Latin *cardo*, hinge)—The four virtues of prudence, justice, fortitude, and temperance are seen as cardinal because all other moral virtues are dependent upon them. At least from the time of Aristotle they were emulated; the Stoics taught and expanded them. Embraced by Ambrose, they were further developed by Thomas Aquinas. The four cardinal virtues were held to be distinct from the "theological virtues" of faith, hope, and love, as more expressive of God Himself. But in Roman Catholic theology, the seven virtues have been conjoined to give direction to what kind of moral person a Christian should seek to see perfected.

Classicism—Aesthetic attitudes and principles based on the teachings of ancient Greek culture and Rome, characterized by an emphasis on form, simplicity, and restrained emotion. (See *Stoicism*.)

Deconstruction—A form of skepticism pioneered by Jacques Derrida that evinces a distrust of modernity's faith in scientific objectivity, reason, and morality. As such, it is a literary form of iconoclasm.

Deism—The belief, based solely on reason, that the creator of the universe set creation in motion and abandoned it, exerting no influence on natural phenomena and providing no supernatural revelation.

Ego—In Freudian thought, an individual's consciousness, operating with secondary processes such as reason, common sense, and the power to delay immediate responses to external stimuli.

Enlightenment—The philosophical movement of the eighteenth century that focused on rational thought and called into question all doctrine and institutions.

Epicureanism—A philosophy developed by Epicurus that denies the afterlife and existence of gods, focusing on the primary emotion of pleasure and freedom from pain.

Ethical—Kierkegaard uses this term in a special way, to contrast the Aesthetic as a lack of social commitment to the freely chosen commitment of an individual's Ethical, or moral, life. But Kierkegaard does not see such outward ethical actions as marriage or baptism as adequately providing one's identity; this he sees as pagan, originating in Aristotle. Indeed, such a viewpoint is close to the morality of the natural law of Aquinas, which he also rejects. For such a life too often leads to a life of conformity, so it belongs to the category of the crowd. (See *Aesthetic*.)

Eudaimonia—The Stoic idea of well-being ("happy spirit") based on the right activity of reason, with a strong emphasis on self-teaching.

Gnostic (Greek *gnosis*, knowledge)—A term coined in the eighteenth century to describe various sects and heresies of earlier periods of Christian history. While their respective myths were diverse, certain beliefs were shared in common: God is unknowable; the material universe was created by a lesser being, or "Demiurge"; human beings have a spiritual part, trapped in matter; salvation is an escape from the material world.

Hegelianism—The thought and diverse influence of Georg Wilhelm Friedrich Hegel (1770–1831), which focuses upon history and logic in which "the rational is the real," and a logic that sees "the truth in the whole." Instead of God taking initiative as Creator, God as "the Absolute Idea" attains self-consciousness through the rationality of humankind. This was the dominant system of thought in Denmark at the time when Kierkegaard was writing.

Heroic—Initially, the Greek hero was an isolated, self-centered figure who lived and died for a personal satisfaction. Associated with *aretê*, human excellence was later attached to civic qualities also; thus service to the state became important, even though self-achievement was glorified. We have used the term to apply more broadly to identify with Kierkegaard's category of the sensual as "aesthetic," to the Greeks' aesthetic appreciation of the human body, gymnastic sports, and the whole metaethical mentoring system associated with Greek culture.

Humanism—A broad term referring to studies of human achievements from Classical and Renaissance to modern times; human pedagogy, the history of the humanistic ideal, with often religious fervor. The Humanist Manifesto of 1933 was drawn up to affirm atheism and pragmatism.

Id—In Freudian thought, an individual's unconscious, associated with the instinctual.

Imago Dei—"The image of God," the Christian doctrine of human beings made in God's image and of sharing characteristics for relationships.

Individualism—The political and social philosophies that place high values upon the individual. These also express that the individual is an end in itself. Society is seen as consisting of a series of individual units, and emphasis is put on self-reliance, privacy, and respect for the rights of other individuals.

Life-view (Danish *Livs-Anskuelse*)—A term adopted by Kierkegaard for a positive attitude to life that takes shape in the course of a society's development, or of a novel's narrative. It is expressive of how a set of values are actually lived out and so gained by experience. From that, Kierkegaard expands upon the possibilities that philosophies that are lived out can provide such life-views, although he is clearly contrasting them with the Christian life-view.

Life-world—An alternative term to Kierkegaard's "life-view," and as a concealed polemic to the modern usage of "worldview," which is more rationalistic and therefore less comprehensive of a metaethical framework of human consciousness and behavior.

Maieutic (Greek *maieutikos,* of midwifery)—Relating to the Socratic method of teaching by eliciting ideas or insights from another, rather than imposing them.

Modernity—Attitudes or forms of thought expressive of modern times. But the period spans from the beginning of the sixteenth century until the 1980s.

Moral—Used loosely to describe Kierkegaard's category of the Ethical. (See *Ethical.*)

Neo-paganism—A loose and negative expression of a modified form of paganism. This can mean a form of polytheism, or can refer to someone with little or no religion or even to a sensual or hedonistic lifestyle.

Objectivism—Any one of various theories asserting the validity of objective phenomena over subjective states and experiences.

Oikeiosis—The Stoic ideal of being self-contained in order to control one's own life and passions. It is essential to know what does and does not depend on us, and of defining the present as what one can control. Thus happiness has to be a present experience. At the same time, there was place for social concern as a higher state of *oikeiosis.*

Paideia—Originally it referred to child rearing in early Greek thought; then it referred to the creation of a higher type of man, suited to carry out the civic duties of city-state. Thus it developed into the idea to foster Greek culture in the pursuit of *aretê.*

Pelagian—Belief in the human being's ability to be righteous by free will, denying the existence of original sin. It is derived from the teachings of Pelagius (ca. 354–418), who blamed Rome's moral laxity upon the doctrine of divine grace. Strongly attacked by Augustine, Pelagius was accused of heresy in 415.

Personalists—Philosophers concerned with the personal character of the human being. There are diverse schools of personalism: Idealist, Realistic Personalist, atheist, Jewish, and Christian. Personalism has been most strongly represented in France during the earlier decades of the twentieth century.

Postmodernity—The modern Cartesian-Kantian worldview, which emphasizes individuality, subjectivity, interiority, and self-subsistent autonomy, has given way to a new sensibility that gives more awareness to the human being as being relational and other-directed. The shock of rationalistic ideologies and their tragic consequences in the modern world have aroused a new social consciousness, together with a new ecological awareness of the interrelatedness of all life forms. Some still prefer to call this "late modern," rather than postmodern.

Psychoanalysis—The "talking cure" developed by Sigmund Freud led him to develop this further into a theory and technique. It assumes a unique relationship between the therapist and client, with a dismantling of previously held opinions by the client as psychoanalysis proceeds. Freud viewed psychoanalysis as a profession that was neither for physicians nor for priests, but a new "science."

Religious, or Religion A—In Kierkegaard's thought, this stage is reached when the two forms of life lived finitely finite—that is, without reference to transcendence or God—the

Aesthetic and the Ethical, lead to despair. Now an alternative, to live in the light of the infinite, of "God," so that "acting absolutely towards absolute ends, and relatively towards relative ends," introduces a "God-relationship."

Religion B—This is the Christian life, with its awareness of personal sin, of personal accountability to the claims of God, and of personal commitment to a living faith in Christ.

Seven virtues—The four Stoic "cardinal virtues" (prudence, justice, fortitude, and temperance) redeveloped during the late Middle Ages in conjunction with the three "theological virtues" (faith, hope, and love), that claimed to be a comprehensive moral identity of those seeking the way of perfection. (See *Cardinal virtues*.)

Stoicism—One of the loftiest and most sublime moral systems of philosophy as a "way of life," developed by the classical world. Virtue and reason are both held to be inherent in the world, no less inexorable than the laws of nature. Perception was believed to be the basis of true knowledge. Man's essential worth, his capacity to control his passions, and his ability to exercise a moderate way of life have all had lasting influences in Western civilization. Stoicism's insistence on the worth of the individual still gives it strong appeal.

Subjectivism—A theory that limits knowledge to subjective experience.

Superego—In Freudian thought, the internalized unconscious "moral principle" that promotes conscience; associated with social conditioning and civilization.

Therapeutic—A generic term for therapy and counseling, which has claimed to be all-embracing of human needs and is in that sense a "religion" or a secular substitute for "religion." It is a metaethical mentoring system that has a health-conscious behavior that involves individual as well as social health.

BIBLIOGRAPHY

Anderson, J. R. L. *The Ulysses Factor*. London: Hodder & Stoughton, 1970.

Annas, Julia E. *Hellenistic Philosophy of Mind*. Berkeley and Los Angeles: University of California Press, 1992.

Augustine. *Confessions*. Vol. 7. Edited by Albert Cook Outler. *The Library of Christian Classics*. Edited by John Baillie, John T. McNeill, and Henry P. Van Dusen. Philadelphia: Westminster Press, 1960.

Barrett, William. *Death of the Soul: From Descartes to the Computer*. New York: Doubleday, 1986.

Battles, Ford Lewis, editor. *The Piety of John Calvin*. Grand Rapids: Baker, 1978.

Bernard of Clairvaux. *On the Song of Songs*. Translated by Kilian Walsh. Kalamazoo, MI: Cistercian Publications, 1981.

Bockmuehl, Klaus. *Listening to the God Who Speaks.* Colorado Springs: Helmers and Howard, 1990.

Bonhoeffer, Dietrich. *Letters and Papers from Prison.* Edited by Eberhard Bethge. Translated by Reginald H. Fuller. London: SCM, 1953.

Bouwsma, William J. *John Calvin, a Sixteenth Century Portrait.* New York: Oxford University Press, 1988.

Brueggemann, Walter. *The Creative Word: Canon as a Model for Biblical Education.* Philadelphia: Fortress Press, 1989.

Calvin, John. *Institutes of the Christian Religion.* Vol. 20 and 21. Edited by John T. McNeill. *The Library of Christian Classics.* Edited by John Baillie, John T. McNeill, and Henry P. Van Dusen. Philadelphia: Westminster Press, 1960.

Cessario, Romanus. *The Moral Virtues and Theological Ethics.* Notre Dame, IN: Notre Dame University Press, 1991.

Come, Arnold B. *Kierkegaard as Theologian: Recovering My Self.* Montreal: McGill-Queen's University Press, 1997.

Connell, George. *To Be One Thing: Personal Unity in Kierkegaard's Thought.* Macon, GA: Mercer University Press, 1985.

Cumming, John. *Letters from Saints to Sinners.* New York: Crossroad, 1996.

Cushman, Philip. *Constructing the Self, Constructing America.* Boston: Addison-Wesley, 1995.

Derrida, Jacques. *Politics of Friendship.* Translated by George Collins. London: Verso, 1997.

Dunn, James D. G. *The Living Word.* Philadelphia: Fortress, 1988.

Edwards, Jonathan. *Religious Affections.* Edited by John E. Smith. New Haven: Yale University Press, 1959.

Ellul, Jacques. *The Humiliation of the Word*. Grand Rapids: Eerdmans, 1985.

Evans, C. Stephen. *Kierkegaard's "Fragments" and "Postscript."* Atlantic Highlands, NJ: Humanities Press International, 1989.

Fénelon, François de. *Telemachus*. Edited and translated by Patrick Riley. Cambridge, England: Cambridge University Press, 1994.

Freud, Sigmund. *Collected Works*. London: Hogarth Press, 1940.

Gellner, Ernest. *The Psychoanalytic Movement*. Evanston, IL: Northwestern University Press, 1996.

Giddens, Anthony. *Modernity and Self-Identity: Self and Society in the Late Modern Age*. Stanford, CA: Stanford University Press, 1991.

Gouwens, David J. *Kierkegaard as Religious Thinker*. Cambridge: Cambridge University Press, 1996.

Homer. *The Odyssey*. Translated by Robert Fagles. New York: Viking, 1996.

Houston, James M. *I Believe in the Creator*. Vancouver, BC: Regent Bookstore, 1998.

Jaeger, Werner. *Early Christian and Greek Paideia*. Cambridge, MA: Belknap Press of Harvard University Press, 1985.

Jenson, Robert W. *America's Theologian: A Recommendation of Jonathan Edwards*. New York: Oxford University Press, 1988.

Kierkegaard, Søren. *Attack upon Christendom*. Translated by Walter Lowrie. Princeton, NJ: Princeton University Press, 1968.

—— *The Concept of Anxiety*. Edited by Reidar Thomte. Princeton, NJ: Princeton University Press, 1980.

———— *Eighteen Upbuilding Discourses*. Edited and translated by Howard V. Hong and Edna H. Hong. Princeton, NJ: Princeton University Press, 1990.

———— *Fear and Trembling; and The Sickness unto Death*. Translated by Walter Lowrie. Princeton, NJ: Princeton University Press, 1974.

———— *For Self-Examination: Judge for Yourself!* Edited and translated by Howard V. Hong and Edna H. Hong. Princeton, NJ: Princeton University Press, 1990.

———— *Journals and Papers*. Edited and translated by Howard V. Hong and Edna H. Hong. Bloomington, IN: Indiana University Press, 1967.

———— *Works of Love*. Translated and edited by Howard V. Hong and Edna H. Hong. New York: Harper, 1967.

Lasch, Christopher. *The Culture of Narcissism*. New York: W. W. Norton, 1978.

Lewis, C. S. *The Abolition of Man*. London: Collins, 1955.

Luther, Martin. *Works*. Weimar edition.

Lyotard, Jean-François. *The Inhuman*. Translated by Geoffrey Bennington and Rachel Bowlby. Stanford, CA: Stanford University Press, 1991.

MacIntyre, Alasdair. *After Virtue*. 2nd ed. Notre Dame, IN: University of Notre Dame Press, 1984.

Marion, Jean-Luc. *God Without Being*. Translated by Thomas A. Carlson. Chicago: University of Chicago Press, 1995.

Masson, Jeffrey M. *The Assault on Truth: Freud's Suppression of the Seduction Theory*. New York: Farrar, Straus and Giroux, 1984.

———— *A Hundred Years of Therapy and the World is Getting Worse*. New York: Farrar, Straus and Giroux, 1985.

McFadyen, Alistair. *The Call to Personhood*. Cambridge, England: Cambridge University Press, 1990.

Meeks, Wayne A. *The Origins of Christian Morality: The First Two Centuries*. New Haven: Yale University Press, 1993.

Meilaender, Gilbert. *The Theory and Practice of Virtue*. Notre Dame, IN: University of Notre Dame Press, 1981.

Menninger, Karl. *Whatever Became of Sin?* New York: Hawthorn Books, 1973.

Mol, Hans. *Identity and the Sacred*. Oxford: Oxford University Press, 1976.

Noll, Richard. *The Jung Cult*. Princeton, NJ: Princeton University Press, 1994.

Nussbaum, Martha C. *The Therapy of Desire*. Princeton, NJ: Princeton University Press, 1994.

Owen, John. *Sin and Temptation*. Edited by James M. Houston. Minneapolis: Bethany, 1996.

Ozment, Steven. *The Age of Reform 1250–1550*. New Haven: Yale University Press, 1980.

Ricoeur, Paul. *Oneself as Another*. Translated by Kathleen Blamey. Chicago: University of Chicago Press, 1992.

Rieff, Philip. *The Triumph of the Therapeutic*. New York: Harper & Row, 1966.

Rogers, Carl. *On Becoming a Person*. Boston: Houghton Mifflin, 1961.

Schoenfeldt, Michael C. *Prayer and Power: George Herbert and Renaissance Courtship*. Chicago: University of Chicago Press, 1991.

Sevenster, Jan N. *Paul and Seneca*. Leiden, The Netherlands: E. J. Brill, 1961.

Steiner, George. *Real Presences*. Chicago: University of Chicago Press, 1989.

Sykes, Stephen. *The Identity of Christianity*. Philadelphia: Fortress Press, 1984.

Taylor, Charles. *Sources of the Self: The Making of the Modern Identity*. Cambridge, MA: Harvard University Press, 1989.

Vanhoozer, Kevin J. *Is There a Meaning in This Text?* Grand Rapids: Zondervan, 1998.

Vardy, Peter. *Kierkegaard*. London: HarperCollins, Fount, 1996.

Vitz, Paul. *Man and Mind: A Christian Theory of Personality*. Hillsdale, OH: Hillsdale College Press, 1987.

Von Balthasar, Hans. *On Prayer*. Urs/Translated by A. V. Littledale. London: SPCK, 1973.

—— *The Heart of the World*. Translated by Erasmo S. Leiva. San Francisco: Ignatius Press, 1979.

—— *Mysterium Paschale: The Mystery of Easter*. Translated by Aidan Nichols. Edinburgh: T. & T. Clark, 1990.

Webster, Richard. *Why Freud Was Wrong: Sin, Science, and Psychoanalysis*. New York: HarperCollins, 1995.

Zizioulas, John D. *Being as Communion*. Crestwood, NY: St. Vladimir's Seminary Press, 1985.

ABOUT THE AUTHOR

Dr. James M. Houston has been a Christian mentor for more than fifty years. A graduate of Edinburgh University and Oxford University, he taught at Oxford University for twenty-three years as a university lecturer and also was a Fellow of Hertford College. After being the founding principal and chancellor of Regent College in Vancouver, British Columbia, he is still there as the Board of Governors Professor of Spiritual Theology. Houston has written *I Believe in the Creator* and *The Heart's Desire* (Regent College Bookstore) and *The Transforming Power of Prayer* (NavPress), and he is the editor of *Classics of Faith and Devotion* (Bethany).

Dr. Houston lives with his wife, Rita, in Vancouver. They have four children and nine grandchildren.

www.ingramcontent.com/pod-product-compliance
Lightning Source LLC
Chambersburg PA
CBHW030304100426
42812CB00002B/551